A Guard

'Sarah Ferguson has written an intensely moving account of her experience of psychoanalysis and of her relationship with her analyst, who suddenly died before her treatment with him was completed. She clearly felt that he was the only person who had ever really accepted and understood her, and her love for him was correspondingly sincere and deep. To interpret such feelings as nothing but "transference" is to miss the point. The grossly deprived cannot repeat experiences which they have never had. Sarah Ferguson's love was genuine because she felt, probably for the first time, that someone really cared for her.'

Anthony Storr

Sarah Ferguson published one other book: *To the Place of Shells* (1975). Before she committed suicide she also wrote a third volume of autobiography which remains unpublished.

Sarah Ferguson

A Guard
Within

Flamingo
Published by Fontana Paperbacks

First published by Chatto & Windus 1973
Published in Penguin Books 1976

This Flamingo edition
first published in 1987
by Fontana Paperbacks
8 Grafton Street, London W1X 3LA

Flamingo is an imprint of
Fontana Paperbacks, part of
the Collins Publishing Group,

Made and printed in Great Britain by
William Collins Sons & Co. Ltd, Glasgow

In the trust of Dr Frey

Durch alle Wesen reicht der eine Raum:
Weltinnenraum. Die Vögel fliegen still
durch uns hindurch. O, der ich wachsen will,
ich seh hinaus, und in mir wächst der Baum.

Ich sorge mich, und in mir steht das Haus.
Ich hüte mich, und in mir ist die Hut.
Geliebter, der ich wurde: an mir ruht
der schönen Schöpfung Bild und weint sich aus.

One space spreads through all creatures equally –
inner-world-space. Birds quietly flying go
flying through us. O, I that want to grow,
the tree I look outside at's growing in me!

I have a house within when I need care
I have a guard within when I need rest.
The love that I have had! – Upon my breast
the beauty of the world clings, to weep there.

RAINER MARIA RILKE

You did die. We talked so often of your dying, and you were determined not to, not just yet. But you did die. Nearly four months ago, and I still cannot believe it. Most people do not want to talk about death and mourning. I want to talk of it all the time because you are the person who I have loved the most, and you have died. I know all about the outer world of social responsibility, so no one can accuse me of continuing to grieve for you. You did not wish to leave your wife and your daughter and your brother, and some of your colleagues and friends. You did not wish to leave me either, and I do not know how to live without you. You knew it would be so.

You had not intended to take a proper holiday this year, but in August you were forced to rest. It was the end of a London summer which had been filled with fatigue and worries and too much work. You would have continued, but you could not. You went with your wife to your house in the west country. I know it only from your descriptions. It is a small house; you said like a hut. It stands above the sea and the cliffs on a hill where scrub-oaks grow. The country is wild. You planted shrubs round the house and on the hill. You took flowering currant and buddleia from the gardener at the hospital and planted them in the spring. The bracken always annoyed you. It grew so fast in the summer and smothered your plants while you were away. That was how you found it when you arrived. You had arranged for it to be kept, but people are not always reliable. You started to work, cutting the bracken on the hill. You worked and worked, and refused to leave some for another day. It was at the end of August, and you came upon a wasp's nest. I was told that as you started away from it up the hill, your heart gave out, and in a few minutes you had died amongst the grass and the bracken which you had scythed. Your wife was by your side.

I start with your death because it is a beginning.

It was March 1968, when I first met you at St Agnes's consulting suite. I noticed that you did not shake hands, but English people very often don't. Otherwise I did not notice you very much. I believe you knew I hated psychiatrists but I went to see you quite willingly because you were a child psychiatrist and I had come about Larissa, who is my adopted daughter and responsibility. I sat looking out of the window at the sky above the Park, and listened to your voice. It sounded quiet and also young, although you were not young. You spoke slowly. You talked of Larissa, and of Maria and Richard, two of my oldest friends who were looking after her for me, and who had brought her to see you because she was crying so at night. After Martin had left me in the autumn they had taken her to live with them, even though they have four children of their own.

Martin left me for a German girl. He is half Dutch. Larissa is Czechoslovakian and French. You are English.

I was living in a furnished flat in Ennismore Gardens. I said it was too small for Larissa as well. You said people live in very small spaces with children. I knew that, you need not have told me. Poor Larissa, she is my duty. I feel so unhappy for her. I became ill in the flat in Ennismore Gardens and was sent to a nursing home by Dr Andrews who drugs one nearly to death. I had been out of there for a week, when I met you.

You asked me if I always looked like a dying duck in a thunderstorm. That made me laugh and laugh. When I reminded you two years later, you seemed surprised and slightly shocked.

It was three o'clock when I arrived and it was five o'clock when I left. You asked me to see you again after the Easter holiday. Nothing had been decided, surely very little achieved and not much conveyed. But I wept all the way back and have longed ever since to live our first meeting over and over again.

*

I did return to see you at St Agnes's. In April and also in May. You had talked to Dr Andrews on the telephone. He had said that, in his opinion, I would always leave Larissa in the most convenient place I could find. I did not feel that you approved of Dr Andrews.

I had been to visit Maria and Richard. On the staircase, when there was nobody there, I had picked Larissa up and held her in my arms. She told me that she knew who I was, although then she could not talk very much. I told her that I loved her.

When I saw you in May, it was the day before I went into Moorfields Eye Hospital for an operation. You said that you were sorry about my eyes. I pretended it was nothing. That day I told you about my baby, and why I had had an abortion. It would have damaged other lives. I had killed my own real baby ten years before, but it remains my living child, and will always be so. It is worse when there is no grave. I wanted you to recognize its existence. No one else does, and that is what I cannot bear.

I walked back under a cloud which had burst, and the rain ran down my face. Why did you affect me so?

That night I went to a party. It was the last I ever went to. I took some purple hearts and danced before going to the hospital. Drinamyl in quantities still work the next day, and I managed to have drinks in the Ritz before lunch with some people I had met the night before. I do not want any of that life, now I have met you.

You telephoned when I got to Moorfields. You said things would be all right, and that you would see me when I came out of hospital. I could not understand why you should be concerned. I told you that I could never abandon Larissa or anyone, I hoped.

You know we spoke of Martin and of Thomas. (I did not give Thomas a name at that time.) But in the months which followed we talked so endlessly of them, and I think I'm too tired to experience it all again. To relive my life on paper hurts too much. It is like an illness. I only wish to speak of you. Now, perhaps, I shall have to tell Dr Frey of the things that have been so precious to me. Otherwise I may just as well not be here in Switzerland. I hope you would agree.

After three weeks in Moorfields, I returned to you at your

hospital. I still had one eye to look at you behind my dark glasses. You did not seem like the doctors in Harley Street, although I knew you had at one time practised there. You did not offer cigarettes from smart boxes, or have ashtrays on stands in your room. You wore a brown suit and not city clothes. You were not huge like the doctors in Harley Street, who perhaps do not care very much, under their desks and their floral arrangements. You were small with a lot of white hair, and your room was bare.

You had hoped these few visits would have been enough, but you now saw it was not the case. For a time, would I come to your flat four days a week? 'Yes,' I said. Maria and Richard had been there to talk about Larissa. They had said that their parents would have thought it nice. I was now going to see for myself. You told me that your flat was hard to find, and you wrote me instructions. I copy them from your paper. 'Opposite National Hall. To top floor, through swing doors, and straight on, to the end.'

*

It is not easy for me to write of this time, the day that I first went to your flat. Now, I will never go there again; but that is no reason to run away. Please help me to stay.

Your flat was in a large Victorian block. There are porters at the door. I did not take the lift. I climbed the stairs. There are flights and flights of red linoleum stairs. I reached the fifth floor and the swing doors. Behind the doors, this is what I saw. A great well in the building, hemmed in by brick walls, is spanned by a passage-way, a bridge suspended in air. There are railings to enclose you but the drop below is so many hundred feet on either side. I never felt safe crossing. Often it would have been easier to fall. But that first time I shut my eyes and afterwards combed my hair. The building is like a prison, or a tenement, or poverty in New York, and pigeons sit on the ledges of the windows in the walls.

You had been working at another hospital all the day. I dressed up for you, and hoped that you would not know.

No, at this moment I cannot describe your flat. It all seems to be too much. It is close, yet inaccessible, and for the time being you have shut me out. Please allow me to return, oh, please do not send me away.

I will turn to my German. I am trying to learn German now, and this is how I begin. Das Zimmer, die Tür, das Fenster, usw. I must go on. Schwarz, blau, weiss, usw.

The room in which I sit has no colour. No colour at all.

Your room was small. There was a grand piano in that room. There was a large cupboard in the room. The cupboard was tall and made of oak. In the room there were two armchairs. The chair on which you sit is by the desk. The desk is by the window. The window is high up. The view through the window panes is broad. The view is of the sky and of buildings. There are plants on the window-sill. Three long bookshelves are full of books. Many pictures hang on the walls. You painted the pictures.

It is a relief just to write of you, who are the dead.

*

I went at five o'clock to see you, except for Wednesdays and week-ends. On Wednesdays you worked late at the hospital. The bus I caught was a 73, although number 9 goes there too. I liked to sit on the hot seats of the buses, or to stand in the rush-hour, thinking of you. It was the greatest pleasure of my day.

The porters at the door began to look at me with suspicious hostility. You said they were a little bit stupid, and might consider that the rates should be raised if they saw me using the lift – although I walk. So often I took the back entrance and climbed up the labyrinthine ways.

I always dressed up for you, and hoped that you would not know. I sat stiffly in my chair, noticing you. Your chair could spin round but you did not use that much; you just occasionally turned it about. I looked more at your books than at you. Jung, Freud and Melanie Klein, Anna Freud, Adler and Rycroft. *Games People Play* and *The Poor World* always caught my eye. I think that Beethoven's letters belonged in another room where I had to wait one day. You were interviewing a woman who was applying for a job in the hospital and who had kept you late.

But you had not engaged her because she had been 'too eager to save'.

I never saw your wife, although I wondered about her. I heard footsteps outside your room, but for months they remained anonymous. I refused to ask you about them. Larissa was our subject. But now that I was seeing her once a week I asked if we should not end our appointments. Yet I told you I was dreading the empty Wednesdays more and more, and my chair had become too small. You gave me a larger chair, and said that you expected me on Wednesdays at six o'clock. I spent the summer evenings secretly dreaming of you, and lived in your life, and not in my own.

*

I had Larissa back at the end of July and took her to Scotland. You gave me your address in the country and the telephone number of some people in the village, who would give you a message if necessary. You were not on the telephone then. You also gave me an address in Switzerland, where you would be spending a few days. I think it was for a conference. I was afraid of leaving you. I was afraid of returning to Scotland too, with the memory of Martin and the previous unhappy year.

I had found Jeanne for Larissa. I avoided them much of the time, but I still had to be conscientious. Beach picnics and more beach picnics, driving, and talking in French – they were like guests who needed entertaining. Once I spoke to you on the telephone, but I was so lonely for you, in spite of the letters we wrote. It was bad luck for you having to write on your holiday, but you did. I spent as much time as I could in the garden with my cat. You knew about my Abyssinian cat, and that she had had kittens, and that I cared for them almost more than people. You knew that one kitten had disappeared, and that I still could not talk of him. He was a cat with a tail like a fox, who behaved like a clown. That summer I saw a pine marten in front of the house. I was watching from the window. It walked slowly at mid-day across the garden steps, and away into the rosebushes. I loved it all so. But there were the things which Martin had begun, and which remained unfinished.

Martin came to stay. I looked forward with apprehension to his coming. He arrived with a basket of live doves, and an antique dancing doll, and a miniature chair for Larissa. We had such a lovely time. I enjoyed being with Larissa and pretended that she was mine. Martin enjoyed it too, for four days. Then he said he was going away, and I realized that none of it had been true. I had allowed myself the game but it was over. He was returning to the German girl, and wished things to stay as they were. He thought that everything had just been nice.

It was the beginning of September and the last night Martin was there. I felt that the house was falling down on top of me. You were in Zürich, but I was afraid of being ill, and so I rang your number. The hotel said that you were out, but you had left the telephone number of the restaurant you were dining in. I did not understand why you had done so and neither did Martin. You did not sound at all surprised to hear me, but the restaurant was noisy, and you were talking in a place where waiters were running in front of you with plates. I cannot remember what we said between Scotland and Zürich, but when Martin left the next day, he felt assured that I was not ill.

Then I began to think about how ignorant of everything I am.

*

During the summer in Scotland I thought all the time of you, and also of the hospital. I do not think of the hospital as much now as I did then. But it was not long after the night when I had to run away from the flat in Ennismore Gardens. Everything appeared to me as being grey, shadowy and still. I was grasped by an iciness.

I went straight to the Casualty Department of St Agnes's. The nurse asked me for my name, address and religion. There were young doctors on duty, like students, and I told them I could not stay at home. They said that I could not stay there. There was nothing wrong with me, and accidents would be coming in. I agreed with them but I would not move. They said I must go to my family or friends, or failing them, the police. I knew they could not take in layabouts, but I was not going to go. I sat shivering on a chair, and the doctors grew sarcastic and aggressive and purposefully tough. They did not know how desperate I was, and that I was not going to go. They were like the front line enemy, and I had got to break them down. After about one hour, a young Chinese doctor became sensible, and allotted me a cubicle for casualties and accidents. So far only, have I been fortunate not to be one of those. The cubicle was bare, and the bed was made of steel, and I felt safe. I slept the night in St Agnes's with delight.

In the morning they treated me like a case, and took me to a department for the disturbed and insane. I told the secretary there that I went to see you. That I went to see you every day. She nearly told me that I was a liar, but instead she said, it could not be so. 'He's a child psychiatrist.' I saw a psychiatrist who was perfectly polite, and who let me go. I was very dirty and battered when I went into the street and the sun.

You asked me why I had not gone to the hospital nearer to where I lived. You asked me why I had not telephoned you. I told you that it had been three o'clock in the morning. You said that would have been little trouble, compared to what it took (and it turned out to be days) to sort it out with the department.

The young doctors said: 'People like you waste other's time. You are guilty.' I was guilty, which is why I have failed to record it in chronological order. You knew, though, why I had to go to the hospital that night.

*

Pasternak wrote: 'I am always astounded to see that what is laid down, ordered, factual, is never enough to embrace the whole truth, that life always brims over the rim of every vessel.' That is the reason I find it so hard to write to you. It is why it is almost impossible, and it is what gives me so much pain. At the time of day when I start to write, I find excuses to turn away to easier things. Each word and every sentence is like a dart under my skin, and because of this each time could be the last. But my spirit will be for ever so close to yours, that I am driven to lay down, order, and make factual, all that I can. I am helpless to do more.

16

You certainly would remember that the autumn was not good. I gave you so much trouble. The summer days which had been beautiful that year had gone. Things had changed. I realized you were a psycho-analyst, and that you were psycho-analysing me. You had not told me that, and I did not like it. I was not a patient. I was just an ordinary proper person. I was cross, I was furious. I resented you, although I did not show it. I was determined not to be caught like a bird in a cage and tamed. But in the autumn I got back to your room where I so wanted to be, where I thirsted to be, and I found that I was trapped. You always let me go of course, but you now knew I would come back, and I did, I had to, and I hated it. Every day I sat for one hour in my chair without saying a word. You sat and waited, unembarrassed. You did not seem to mind but you said that it was a waste of money, and often we did get tired towards the end. You put a clock on the chimney-piece. It had a very loud tick, and I asked you to take it away. I never saw it again.

One day I could stand it no longer. I turned my back on you, and put my arms around my chair and held it very tightly. I could not see you, but I sensed your movement. It was so quick that it was as though you had not moved at all. I felt your hands upon me. You held me firmly in your hands. You had never touched me before, and it made me snap like a branch into two, and I began to trust you to put me together. You started to take off my coat when I came into the room. Before, I had kept it on. And now when I left, you would fasten up the buttons. I never liked the leaving. I always lingered and stood around. I would look at you in the glass which hung behind my chair. It was quite a pretty looking-glass with a carved bird on the top, but you had not hung it properly, and the picture-hook showed on the wall. I did not touch anything, but as I walked slowly down the passage I shuffled my feet and ground them into your carpet, until I reached the front door. You never closed the door quickly. You waited until I was some way down the stairs.

I was living then in Cadogan Lane with Larissa and Jeanne. The house was built of grey cardboard and furnished in plastic, and its smallness and lack of privacy sent me mad. You asked me why I chose that expensive area, and one which was so near to Martin. Well, it was taken for me while I was in Scotland, and I had to have somewhere to put Larissa on our return. Larissa went to a respectable little nursery school which she enjoyed, and there was Millie who came by day to take her out for walks, and there was Jeanne there at night to put her to bed. And Mrs Watson came to cook the lunch. I took Larissa to the dancing class on Thursdays. I hated the dancing class with the mothers and nannies. I hated the school with the mothers and fathers. I would not go to the school. After some weeks we did not go to the dancing class because Larissa started to spit, and blow bubbles and foam at the mouth. She enjoyed the dancing class too. Poor little Larissa. But I would not be stared at by that upper-class dancing school.

There was my birthday. I still minded about that. I took Larissa and Jeanne out to lunch in a restaurant. Martin sent me a picture but I did not see him. The picture was of Neapolitans gazing at a Crucifix with what looked like Mount Etna, but must have been Vesuvius, behind them.

I spent all the days wandering. I would not go back to the depression of that house until after I had seen you in the evening. I explored the ground all round where you lived. I liked the North End Road. It was the wrong end, where the greengrocer sold bad fruit, and the junk shop labelled elegant but out-dated shoes at five shillings a pair. The Hammersmith Road is always very dirty, with bits of paper scattered everywhere. The newspaper delivery boys fight outside the fish and chip shop and the pub which has Courage written in huge letters on the roof. There is always a show on at the National Hall. The Dairy Show, the Poultry Show, the International Packaging Show, etc. I never went to one, except in order to go to the lavatory because I did not want to ask you. The lavatory is extremely difficult to find in the National Hall. My difficulty was to arrive, for you, exactly on time. It was growing cold, so if I got there early I would stand in the news-agent's shop along the road. I bought envelopes and postcards, and pretended to consider the plastic souvenirs and the paper-back novels which tried to deal with sex. I made friends with the man who owned the shop, and he let me read the *Evening Standard* while I watched his clock. His daughter never liked me. I think she thought I was a prostitute, waiting around like that. I bought cigarettes there too, and hid them in the bottom of my bag. I did not admit to you for ages that I smoked several cigarettes a day. I think if you had smoked I might not have returned to you. But I really do not know the reason why.

*

I have said already that the autumn was not good. I have said that I gave you trouble. You guided me into the troubles, and it does not interest me to write of them. Egoism, Narcissism, I, The Subject. Must I tell you all . . . and the trivialities?

If I had not met you, I would be dead, or perhaps in hospital, or even getting around with a polite smile on my face. Faking 'mother' to Larissa, and pretending to keep house, and remaining in circulation with my friends. Instead I write down Egoism, Narcissism, I, The Subject, and You. The Subject is not I, neither is it you. The Subject is, life for everything.

You telephoned me every evening. I was very grateful to you. Sometimes we would talk for five or ten minutes, and sometimes for three-quarters of an hour. I liked to be in my bed before you rang at ten o'clock, and I always asked if everything was all right. Of course things were not, and never will be all right, but you were all right with me. That is what matters throughout the whole of the world. 'You are all right with me.'

I did not quite trust you though. I thought that you might be pretending, like doctors do.

I swallowed ten sodium amytal one evening before you telephoned. I always think of Larissa, and of everything that I should, but there is always the step which can lead beyond. You suggested that I drink some salt and water or put my finger down my throat. I did as I was told but it did not work, and I did not really care any more. I went to sleep chancing it, and I woke the following evening, just in time to go to see you. I swayed down your passage, falling from side to side, with shaking legs. You sent me back in a taxi, in case I got run over in the Hammersmith Road. After that you gave me my sleeping pills every night, in my pocket or in a brown envelope. But only because I asked you if you would. You said that if I were determined to die, you could not stop me. You said that you would 'go through the mill' but that you would get over it in the end.

Gerard died from nembutal. Bad, bad Gerard. He was my friend.

*

You had some small pottery pots on the top of your bookshelves. After a time I had to ask you to put them away. They became irresistible. To smash. I have always broken things. My own prettiest things of which I have taken such care. Even as a child I knew how destructive I was, and I used to watch myself as I broke people and situations and relationships I loved. I have broken all the things I have loved the most. Sometimes you have a hand in the fate which you receive, and I know where my sins have come in. They terrify, and make me cry, because I do not want to break the world.

I am so gentle, and so good and so nice. I have always taken everybody in. I think you really hated me when I was like that. You found me nauseating, I think.

Everyone fears catastrophes and disasters and crashes and deaths, and people who attack you in the dark. You made all that worse for me. I felt something might happen which would separate me from you, and I could not deal with life without you. I would not stand about in crowds, in case a knife should be stuck through my back. And if I saw an Arab sitting in the bus, I would get off in case he had a bomb. One evening I had climbed your stairs and was going the open air way. Through the swing doors I met a man with an apron on. He was not ordinary.

He took me by the arm, although he was very small. 'Knives or scissors to be sharpened?' was what he said.

I ran down your passage-way. I was covered in a cold sweat. You said it was a coincidence, and I could see that in fact you were amused. I shall never be amused by the thought of that little sharpener, standing in the alley.

Once, late at night, I left Cadogan Lane without telling Jeanne I was going. I was free, and I had a hammer and a brick in my hands. I had often tried to get out of your room, having travelled all the way there. It frightened me to be caught in a trap which was becoming painful, and one from which I had no escape. I pulled the brass handle of your door, and reached up to the glass at the top, but you always stopped me, and you were very strong. I am strong too. Now I was going to smash the glass in your front door, and break you and me, once and for all. When eventually I arrived, my plan went wrong. I found that I was foiled. The porters lock the street doors at eleven o'clock. 'You stupid little fool. Go back to where you belong.' That is what I said. And I did go. But I did not belong.

A straight romance. That was what you said of what you had been to me that summer. I did not mind. I will think and feel exactly as I please. I know you were not mocking me.

In spite of all the troubles, I drove you to distraction with my good behaviour, and what you called my idealization of you. You wanted me to be nasty and bad-tempered and rude, but I was not, and I was not going to please you.

I had a dream that you had a letter from your daughter. It was very brightly coloured, and covered in flowers. She said: 'I love you very, very much. I do not seem to see much of you, though, these days.' I did not like it that you had a letter from your daughter; but I don't believe you did see much of her those days.

One day after many troubles, you led me to a different room, and lay me down on a bed. It was dark except for a light above my head. The light glowed red very dimly because it was covered over with paper. The pillow-case on the pillow was new and clean. You spread a rug over me and sat beside me on a little chair. I saw a shelf crowded with ornaments directly above my head. They must have been your daughter's ornaments. It must have been your daughter's room. I was in it now, and they had become my ornaments. They were mine, like the ornaments which Nan always gave me for every occasion. I thought of Nan, sitting beside me with the light covered over, and playing cat's cradles or noughts and crosses when I was ill.

Then I saw you playing with a piece of string. You wound it round and round your finger, and I expect you were not thinking of very much.

'What are you doing?'

'Oh nothing, just silly twiddling. I was not thinking,' you said.

You sat occupied beside me, but you were there. There are few sweeter pleasures than that. I liked being in the room with the ornaments, and I liked it when you wrapped my feet up in the rug. Tactile. That was the word you used. You would not allow things to become too tactile. There was an evening when I saw sewing things on the table. I saw the reels of cotton through the dark. I looked at you and asked you whose they were.

'Whose do you think?' you replied.

I knew that your daughter was away at school, and I knew that they belonged to your wife, but I was not going to tell you.

'Do you love me? Do you love me like a daughter?' I was always asking you that.

'I love you like a daughter.'

'You're pretending.'

'I could not do what I do for you, if I did not,' you said.

*

I feel so depressed in Zürich today, and so lonely for you. I wish to God I knew how I am going to see it through. Often I wonder if it is self-torture I am inflicting on myself, but I do not think that you would have thought it so. I ask you for courage, and for how long will I have to go on without you?

I will think now of your picture in the room where the ornaments were. It was one that I particularly like. You had painted it in the Cotswolds, twenty years before. It is of flowers, but I thought that they were weeds. It was not really painted very well. It was a nice little picture though, the weeds in the Cotswolds. It was full of happiness.

My times in the room with the ornaments did not last very long. One day I saw the porters carrying a trunk. They arrived on your doorstep at the same time as myself, and they made a lot of fuss heaving it about. 'This way . . . no, that way. Is she in, or is she out?' I did not know where to go. How clumsy the porters were, in their peaked caps. Did they not know that they were trampling on my ornaments? In your room, I stood with my face towards the cupboard. I would not speak to you. Your daughter had come back from school. You said you were sorry, and that you wished you had another room. But nothing would have made it any better.

There is the outer and the inner world. Only the inner is alive for me. Nothing can take that away. Reality consists of both the worlds. They are separated by a very fine partition, which your daughter with her ornaments had broken through. I cried for two hours with my face towards the cupboard. Then I went away, and caught the bus.

I look again at your painting of the weeds. In the outer world it is mine now, and I wish it were not so. Oh, please help me to deal with Zürich.

Since I last wrote, I have been sent away from the Klinik. That is not quite correct because I had a choice. To stay at the Klinik as a living-in patient, or not go back there at all. It was because of the breaking. I smashed a table and some ashtrays into bits, and I tore Dr Frey's suit. You would not approve of that, and nor do I. I respect other people's property. I am extremely sorry for what I did. I wrote to Dr Pestalozzi, the director. I do not like people with bad manners.

I broke them all up because they belonged to Dr Frey. I cannot bear it that you are no longer here, and my only hope is to stay close to him. I know that is no explanation so I will just have to leave it as it is. It was yesterday that I would not leave the room after Dr Frey had gone. I wanted to feel again his presence, for one second, to enable me to go on. I know that it was childish, but it was true. I know he is very busy, and cannot bend to every whim. I knew I was being difficult and wanting too much. But I want; and I am difficult; and I wish that I were not. Finally they tried to hound me out and I got fierce. I think I may have bitten Dr Carlton. You knew I never liked him, but that is no excuse. They put me to bed with sleeping medicine.

Dr Frey came and told me that either I stay at the Klinik, or do not go there at all and see him in his office instead. It was, I suppose, perfectly fair. There are many people who have to be considered in the Klinik. I have always known that. Dr Frey is a good and an honourable man. From him, though, it tasted like the most bitter pill.

You know what I feel about the Klinik. There are many people I love there, although I do not talk to them much. I have hated the Klinik, but I have wanted to return to it in the end. One is safe there. I agreed with Dr Frey to talk about it later, but it was not to be like that.

In the evening, Frau Dr Holz came to see me. She held a pencil and paper in her hand, and wished to know immediately whether I was going to sign and stay. I wonder if she knew how much it took from me, that I would not sign and stay? But now it is so necessary for me to write to you, and to have my own base to struggle from. I may well not succeed, I know that. Frau Dr Holz said good-bye and got up to go. I dressed and went down to the hall. I felt more stupid than usual from the sleeping medicine. I put on my coat, and looked for my key to the door. It had gone. I shall not forget that. I do not have to explain to you why, and it had nothing to do with Dr Frey. I could not understand. It had been there in the morning. I told one of the male nurses that my key had been taken from the pocket of my coat. Herr Bürger is a friend. He came to see me when I was in the Kantonsspital. He now laughed, and said that this morning my key might have been in my pocket, but now it was gone. I shall not forget that. It is not simplicity. If they had asked me for the key, I would have given it to them.

Herr Stieler unlocked the door. 'Good night. Sleep well,' was what he said.

I shall not forget it.

Today I cried all day. It is like another catastrophe to be rejected by the Klinik. I mind very much about the Klinik. I felt like going to the station to throw myself under a train. Then I thought, why should I? It is the German in them, and I do not bother about the German in anyone. It hurts, it crushes, and it does not trust, and it kills while it smiles. It is something unique. It is a built-in force, but one which has no true strength. That is why I must not let it crush me. I feel it as I walk the streets, and the tears will go on falling down my face. I feel it bruising and twisting and battering my soul, and I wonder if I can go on. I am not forceed to stay, nobody wants me to stay; except, I wonder, do you?

I am trying and failing to learn the German language. It has so many beautiful words. Protect me though from the hidden German, who can never be my friend.

I like Dr Frey. You knew that. Now I like Frau Frey as well. She gave me milk. I have a very great deal to be grateful to them for. I like their flat too. It is quite like yours. You were very, very English, and I am too; but not insular

Dr Frey told me today that Astrid Stramm at the Klinik has

thrown herself out of the window. She has broken her pelvis and her leg. I do not know her at all, but I know that she has a baby at home. I was in the bed next to her when they put me to bed the other day. She had the strap around her waist. I had the strap round me last autumn. I asked for it to be put there, in case I smashed everything up. I know how terrible it is to be bound, even kindly.

I do not know anything about Astrid Stramm, but I believe I have known how she felt. I am so sick and sad for her today. I am angry also, for that action, which is constantly in my mind, she has presented to me on a plate.

It was raining in Zürich today. Slush was all over the streets. I had no idea where I was going when I left Dr Frey, and I thought I would faint. A young man came out of the house and walked to the gate. I wanted to talk to him or to anybody. I went to a restaurant, but they said it was too late. I woke with a dreadful pain of hunger this morning, but it was not for food. You knew about that. It was our most important secret, and because you knew, it kept me alive.

I went to the restaurant of the Kunsthaus and had some coffee, and thought about Astrid Stramm. I had given you the catalogue of the Kunsthaus when I had returned from Zürich last spring. You were very pleased with it. You had enjoyed visiting the Kunsthaus. As I sat in the restaurant I saw a man come in, and for a moment I thought it was you. I often do that. I wondered whether to go and look at some paintings, to engage with something beautiful, but I could not. I feel that a net is drawing round me here, closer now each day, and I do not know what it means. I am very afraid of being so much alone, but I do not really want people. There is a strain on me which is becoming intense. Astrid Stramm must be in the Kantonsspital. I was there last autumn. I was in Dermatology which is next door to Broken Limbs.

I walked back to my room in the hotel. Everything was there just as I had left it. My books. Harold Nicolson's *Diaries*; a child's book to help me to read in German called *Liebe Welt*; and *Steppenwolf* lies open because I cannot stop reading it, although I do not really know what it means. It, too, makes me afraid. My typewriter is there. It always seems to be waiting for me. The blank sheets of paper are stacked in a neat pile. They are perfectly white and empty. I have bought a *Daily Express* to add something new to the room. There is a postal strike in Britain. All communications are cut. I look at your face, your photographs, which I do so many times a day. I will write to you. I must somehow go on, because I truly love you and do not wish to fail you. Please ask Dr Frey for me, if he could make certain that the net which is drawing round me will not strangle. I do not want to ask him myself.

I would be afraid to visit Astrid Stramm.

When I returned to you after Christmas, two years ago, we slowly began to talk of 'Eleanor', the story which took seventeen years to take shape in my mind. Seventeen years to write fifteen thousand words! She committed suicide, or rather decided to die, in the end. I must not waste seventeen years of fighting with 'Eleanor'. Not all that, for nothing.

You always told me to be kind to myself. Perhaps if I am it might loosen the net? I will, therefore, allow myself to say, I love.

Forgive me for writing with such disorder. I have always hated the verbose.

*

I must try and pick up the pieces today, and return and write to you. It is the only comfort I can find. You and also music. Last night I was writing until three o'clock, and today I am tired. My typewriter has collapsed. You knew a lot about tiredness. I wonder if we knew of the same kind? I suppose every kind comes to the same thing in the end. I will sleep, and start again tomorrow.

As I go to sleep, I want to hold your, or even Dr Frey's hand, and be led up the stairs, or the mountain, or the Jupiter Steig. I hold on very tightly, do not let me fall or let me go. Then suddenly I break away roughly and reach the top long before you. I look at you still climbing slowly up. I am there above you. I am free, and I am strong. It lasts though only one minute. I wish it could always be so. Why does one wear oneself out, longing to be safely held?

How wonderful to greet the morning gladly.

Tomorrow has come and I am still tired, but I am returning to write about Christmas, two years ago. It was the second Christmas that I had hated. It makes me sad to see people hating Christmas, but now I know that it is the pain of homesickness which they hate, and not Christmas itself. One is fortunate to have loved Christmas even once. You were going to the west country. I was going to my sister and her husband and children in Somerset. The children are blond and extremely beautiful, and I feel they are almost mine. I do not really know them, but I love them more than Larissa. I have been afraid to be alone with them, in case I squeezed them to death.

Jeanne had returned to France. She and Larissa were upset. I felt ashamed that I could not look after Larissa myself but I could not. It was true. I got too excited and angry, and might have abandoned her in the house, or some such monstrosity. I found a Miss Kimmins for Larissa. She wore a hearing aid and was not at all suitable. I was supposed to take her and Larissa to my sister for Christmas. I had got to move into another house, and it all made me ill. 'How feeble,' they say.

You arranged for Larissa to go to the children's ward at St Agnes's in South London, providing I went to see her every day, except while I was away. You said she would have a good time at Christmas. The sister of the ward was your friend.

I took Larissa there on the tube. We had to change at Leicester Square. Larissa was wearing her red plastic anorak and her balaclava helmet. I cried inside for her all the way on the tube. It was a very long way, and she started to grumble. The station was ten minutes' walk from the hospital, but it seemed miles and miles. I was carrying her belongings in a bag. She insisted on looking so small and stocky and discontented, and her nose would not stop running. The outside of the hospital resembles a concentration camp with brick chimneys here and there. You did not think much of it yourself. It was so very dismal. It was better when we reached the children's ward. There were Christmas trees and paper-chains, and cotton-wool snow on the window panes. Larissa was interested. She loves Christmas trees. I sat her in a little cot, and fed her lunch with a spoon. I pretended for the other mothers to show them how good I was. Larissa pretended too. She ate all her lunch which usually she does not do. It was turkey, and then jelly and ice-cream. The doctor came to see her, and we pretended she had a cough. The sister of the ward was young and pretty and nice.

I wondered where you were in the hospital.

'I think you should leave now,' said the sister. 'And pay no attention if she cries.'

She did not.

I will continue to tell you about Larissa today, and perhaps get that finished for a time. There are so many other things I would rather write to you about. Your silver pen-tray for instance, in your room. Do you remember that particularly bad Sunday, when you told me to come round? I had to bring Larissa with me because Jeanne was out. You gave Larissa a box of farmyard animals to play with. They were made of lead and were old and very pretty. Larissa was wearing her red mackin-tosh and hat, and she played on the floor. There was a little dove-cote, and she kept trying to put the dove inside. You did it for her. As we left, you told me I had rejected her the whole time. She had got one of your marbles in her hand. I took it from her and put it in my pocket. I just remember that.

The first time I went to see Larissa in the hospital after Christmas, she was pleased to see me. We were put in a room together, and she sat on my lap. We did not talk or play, we just sat. You came in. You had on your coat and hat. I had not expected to see you. I felt embarrassed that you should see me with Larissa on my lap, and I think she was embarrassed too. She was very pleased to see you. You saw her most days when she was in the hospital. She loved you.

The next time I went to see her, I took her for a walk. We went round the tarmac roads of the hospital. It was grey and it was muddy, and the air was filled with fog. She would not come. I found a tree for her which had a thrush on its branch. She stopped crying for a minute, but I had to drag her along.

All the other days I went to see her, she would not look at me. She was wearing the clothes of the hospital, and carpet slippers. She held a toy windmill on a stick and ran about the passages. When I tried to talk to her, she pointed her finger at me, like someone grown-up, and shouted at me to go away. The other mothers looked shocked. I walked past the new-born babies in their incubators, and the heated tank full of tropical fish, and went away. The sister asked you to tell me not to come any more.

I had bought a house off the King's Road, which had a very small garden for my cat. There were the Chelsea Hospital Gardens for Larissa. It was quite an old house, and it had not been spoilt. In fact the roof was falling in. There was a great deal to be done to it. It took many months. I knew that I was very fortunate to be able to buy a house, but I did not want it one bit. I could not take any interest in it whatsoever. I had no furniture. Martin still had it all. You told me to get some beds and a table and to arrange my books. I did.

The sister of the hospital said that she could keep Larissa no longer. She was not ill, and the authorities would start to object. So I had to fetch her away, and she and I and Miss Kimmins moved to my new house. Larissa liked it there, but she hated Miss Kimmins, and I knew that I would have to ask her to go. Larissa sat in her high chair, with tears rolling down her face, while Miss Kimmins shouted because she would not eat her food. I could not bear it for Larissa. I knew exactly how she felt. We felt the same. I promised her that it would not last much longer. I took her into a conspiracy. I told her in the street so that no one would hear. The conspiracy said that we had got to pretend to be happy. She looked relieved and understood.

I will not dwell in Zürich any more. Not for the moment. I will not take notice of the grey streets here, or the loneliness, which follows and follows. I will not see the trams, or the snow which lies half-thawed. Not even the swans on the Limmat. I will walk like someone blind.

I have known for a long time about geography. I could be anywhere in the world; amongst the ruins of Sabratha, or in the marble mountains of Cemtou, but I would not be there. I would be in your room with you.

After Christmas, you did not allow me to return to the room with the ornaments. You were strict. Instead, you took away the picture of the weeds in the Cotswolds from your daughter's room, and hung it over your bookshelves above my chair. You bought a small footstool from a shop in the North End Road, especially for me. It had a green damask covering. Neither of us thought that it was in very good taste, but you were full of pleasure to have found it. It was exactly what you had been looking for. You also added a rose-coloured velvet cushion beside my chair. I did not touch it for a long time. So now I had my chair with the cushion beside it, my footstool, and my rug, and also my picture. The gas fire was always lit, either burning too high or too low. It was never just right. If you came back late from the hospital you used to fumble with the matches and light it, muttering about the cold and telling me to come in. I never entered the room until you had everything straight. You usually made some tea and sipped it out of a mug. You apologized for drinking the tea, and once asked me if I would like some too. But I never drink tea. I was very afraid of making you angry, and I knew where your temper lay. To tread on it was like a catastrophe. I knew that you were really quite a cross person, irritable, and exceptionally fussy, like me. They were characteristics, though, which were not at all obtrusive. Sometimes, as you drank your tea, I would ask for a leaf from your geranium. I would bruise it for its smell and take it back with me on the bus.

I had never talked to you of loving physically. I had decided to hide it behind a stone. I hid it behind a stone for a very long time. I do not like talking.

One day, after many troubles, you were holding me, and my head was just touching your face, and I became stronger than you, and you became mine. I had done nothing, and I did not mean to do it, and I hated to see you at my advantage. My head was only just touching your face. We never spoke of it, either then or at any time, except once you allowed yourself to make a reference in saying almost cryptically, 'And you well know it.' I tell you, it became easier to be with you then (but not noticeably so), and my trust in you grew. That is all.

*

Martin had been to see you twice. The first time he had liked you, and said that you reminded him of a don. The second time he did not like you so much, because you told him that he should go away and not see me for a year. I always wanted to see Martin but every time it was the same. We met on neutral ground in restaurants, our talk going round and round, and always ending with me in tears. He wanted things to remain exactly as they were but I did not see how that was possible. He still had not told his parents that we had been separated for a year and a half. He said it was because they were too old, and the shock to them would be great. I wrote them letters pretending that everything was all right. I asked you if you could find help for Martin, and you arranged for him to see Dr Rogers in Harley Street. Martin went willingly but the visit was not a success. Martin did not like Dr Rogers. He said that he was brusque and rude. Dr Rogers told you that Martin had absolutely no intention or wish to bring about any changes in himself, and that he would have found him an impossible case. I felt sad for Martin because I know that he always believes himself, and what he says, to be true. In many ways I felt responsible for him. I had wanted to marry him for five years before we did, and Martin should never have got married, which I always refused to see. He should be looked after though, and loved. 'Why are you not more of a femme d'artiste?' he says to me. I do not like that expression, not only because I find it affected, but because I do not believe that such a creature exists. Martin thinks I am bourgeoise (when he is angry) but I do not really know what he means, because it is a word which has become so misused.

I had no idea what to do, because I love him. You said that I hated him too. Maybe a little, sometimes, for what he has done to me; but he is like a child who you always forgive. I agreed with you not to see him, and did not for many months, except when I sent him flowers on his birthday, and I met him accidentally in the street. He was wearing one of the white roses in his buttonhole. I did not see him after that. He sent me presents and wrote me letters but I did not answer them. All communications were cut.

It was not you who persuaded me to start divorce proceedings. The action was entirely my own. I was not influenced by anyone. Like Thomas, I have always dreaded divorce. It has not entered my background for generations. If ever. I see it as a murderer, as a divider of what should be whole. But I see it most of all as a broken promise to God. It is not naïve to say that, in this sophisticated world, even to an unbeliever. The question is, why did you kneel before the altar?

This is the psalm I chose for our wedding. It was read by the curate as there was nobody to sing. I like to hear it, and I write it down because it gives me pleasure. I think you would also like it.

'Lucerna pedibus meis: Thy word is a lantern unto my feet: and a light unto my paths. I have sworn, and am steadfastly purposed: to keep thy righteous judgements. I am troubled above measure: quicken me, O Lord, according to thy word. Let the free will offerings of my mouth please thee, O Lord: and teach me thy judgements. My soul is always in my hand: yet do I not forget thy law. The ungodly have laid a snare for me: but yet I swerved not from thy commandments. Thy testimonies have I claimed as mine heritage for ever: and why? they are the very joy of my heart. I have applied my heart to fulfil thy statutes alway: even unto the end.'

*

I have broken the discipline of my day, by sleep. Every day here in Zürich I have to impose a rigid discipline on myself in order not to break, dissolve, and go to pieces. It can be necessary to go through that state in illness; but not now, please not now. To be ill again would stop me from writing to you, and to write to you is more vital to me than food. I am close to you when I write, and I also see again what you taught me. Instead of remaining a ghostly shape, it will for ever take a living form. You would wish this because it was your work.

I had observed from my father and from my mother's family how to be just, and how to be dutiful, and how to fight. To command a regiment is a heavy burden to be landed with, but one which I would not wish to be without.

33

You showed me that a life exists with a living God, and not a dead one. I did not know it before, and still do not know how to grasp that life; or even if I wish to. That is why I must go on writing to you. One day of rest means a day of emptiness for me, a day of frustration, and a loss of hope. I must not lose sight of what you showed me, whatever I may do. We talked about God because I wished to. You were always open and without dogma, even evasive. I suppose because you were wise.

I do not know why it requires such strength to write to you. I get so tired. At the end of the week I am exhausted (having done nothing to an observer) and I have to sleep, and then I lose time. I woke just now with terror of the knowledge that everything is transitory. Everything except for God. To know that is certainly not new to me, but it is why I must not waste time. It is why I must get on with writing to you.

I have always been so afraid of losing you. I do not know how many times I said : 'Please do not die.' Every day I feared that you would leave me, and would take your hand from mine. You assured me it would not be so but I did not believe you. And you let go of my hand which you held, in the open country. I know that it was not your choice. You said that if an analysis was successful, it was forgotten afterwards. In this case it could never have been so. You were not only my guide and teacher. You see, I love you and desire you now, in the outside wintry world in which I stand.

I got out of step again. I must train myself not to do so. Everything must be recorded in its correct time and place. In its chronological order. You said that I spoke in a dialect of my own, which at first you found hard to understand. You taught me to speak more clearly, and I must not relapse into my old instinctive language of disorder.

•

I found Colette for Larissa. She was as neat and cheerful and intelligent as anyone could wish, and Larissa loved her. You came to visit Colette to make things easier for me. It was very kind of you and Colette liked you. You had arranged for Larissa to go to a clinic every afternoon. You said that it would make

34

things better for her and myself. I took Larissa there, the first time. It was a huge modern building in North London. It was made of slabs of stone and concrete, and plate glass. We went to the Department for Parents and Children. I met a psychiatric social worker, who I was to see once a week. She was a friend of yours. Her name was Miss Lane and she was extremely nice. Larissa behaved impossibly. She would not allow me to take off her coat, she screamed when I touched her, and lay down on the floor. She only did that in front of other people. I left her while she played with farmyard animals. New, ugly, constructive ones, made of plastic; not like yours. When I returned, I was told that she had left the poor little pig all alone in the middle. What a sickly way to describe a state of mind. Even for a child. The weak symbolism affronted me. I felt furious. I was in a bad mood in this clinic, with their Department for Marriage Guidance, and Parents and Children. I suspected it was a good place really, and it was free. No financial problems for anyone. You called it by a nickname, so intimately, like a close friend. I wished you would not do that, but I did not say so.

There was the problem of how to get Larissa to North London. Every afternoon, there and back. She was still only three years old, and she never would have stood the long journey, changing buses and tubes. There was much walking involved, and Larissa would not walk; and she also had the nursery school. I found a girl with her own car to take Larissa to the Clinic in the afternoons. I do not approve of silly generalizations, but I hate those countless women in their mini busy cars. Larissa saw a young American woman at the Clinic. I liked her but did not speak to her much. I spoke to Miss Lane every week. I went to that Clinic by bus, changing three times, so that I would not have to go with Larissa and the girl in the car, talking, talking all the way. Once I went with them. It was a mistake. Larissa sat on the back seat, and I sat in front. Suddenly she put her arms tightly around my neck. I screamed and got out of the car. I could not stand the contact, and the proximity. Larissa's driver thought I was evil. I never went with them again.

Round and round the weeks went, like that. You were there. You kept it going. I had a row with the headmistress of Larissa's school. She would not, and could not understand about the Clinic. I have never come across such a person in all my life. She said things to me which may well have been true, but they were inexcusable. I cried all day. You talked to her on the telephone, and you could not get her off the line. She would not let you go for an hour and a half. I saw you at the end of it and you were quite shaken. With all your experience of heads of schools, you had never met one like her. Narrow-minded, snobbish old bitch, charging a huge fee each term for the babies of upper class, and diplomatic, and respectable professional families. And the children were very happy there too. Never would I enter her door again for the Nativity Play, or the Concert or Open Day. I would not inspect Larissa's handiwork, or hear her sing a song, and see her curtsy when she received her prize. I would not look at the happy smiling mothers and proud fathers. I would blow it all up. I was caught in this suffocating circle of domesticity, where I had no place, and no wish to be.

Once I had wanted, just as much as Larissa, for my handiwork to be looked at by my father and mother. I knew what I was doing to Larissa. I could not bear it for her, nor could I make myself go. Larissa did not understand, but she is very understanding. Colette or Mrs Watson would act proxy for me.

Sometimes when at last I reached you, I would be shaking with rage, and I would shout and stampede against the bonds of my confinement. It exhausted me. Often you gave me a glass full of glucose and soda-water, which you would take from your cupboard. I would drink it from your hand in one draught, not able to put it aside, and wait for one moment, so desperately I craved for it. One day, I bit the glass into pieces when I had finished drinking. I was exasperated that there was no more. You were not pleased, and thought you would have to take me to the hospital, but I spat out all the bits into a bowl. The next day I brought you a beautiful wine glass, on a thin stem.

Not long after, I made a comedy. It was neither an amusing nor an interesting one. All of a sudden I decided to make it, and you could not have stopped me. I started at the beginning and finished at the end. I was on a stage and you were in the

36

audience. Your room, the theatre, was very cold, and so was I, the actress, and you were too, sitting down there in the stalls. But at any cost the play had to go on.

I took off all my clothes in front of you. I took them off very slowly, and very precisely. I did it very professionally. You protested to start with, but you saw it was no use because you could not reach me on the stage. I folded my clothes neatly and made a pile of them, as they came off one by one. I stripped myself bare without any gaiety or joy. It was a very good strip-tease, but solemn. I stood like a marble figure, in front of you. When the show was over, and your room became your room, and we were once more sitting in our chairs, I looked at you. We agreed that the performance had been boring.

That night I found my duties even harder to carry out than usual. They were not much. Talking the news of the day with Colette to prevent her from feeling alone, and saying good night to Larissa, who was always waiting for me in the dark. She would never lie down until I came back. There was one thing which induced her to sleep. It was something which was expected of me and I did it. We had to recite the titles of the two pictures in her room.

'All things bright and beautiful,' we said.

And, finally, before I could escape: 'Master Becher on his celebrated pony Lady ...'

'Lady?'

'Bird,' she said.

Then I drank three vodkas in privacy. At that time I never told you about my drinking. I made conversation to someone who telephoned me, and then I waited for your call. Forgive me for my comedy? You said there was no need. The relief to me was immense. The tone of your voice sent me to sleep. It was like the embrace which I should have given to Larissa.

*

Acting-out. That was what you called it. You did not like the vocabulary of your profession. Jargon, you called it. You did not think that acting-out was necessary.

I was either too good or too bad. I was never able to get it right. You did not like me when I was good. When I was bad, you said the upper class word would be 'tiresome', but that that was a word you never used. It must have been trying for you. I touched things in your room. I fluffled your books on their shelves, and when I was angry I pulled them all out. They came crashing down, one on top of the other, on to the floor. I did not mean to hurt your books. I cared for them, and put them back in their right place, every time. I dust my books with a feather duster once a week, and make sure that they do not get warped by too much heat. I have to keep my room quite cold and with enough humidity, because of them. You did not let such things worry you.

I played without mercy. I did not want to wear you out, only to test the limits of your endurance. I made you very tired. I invented games and diversions, so that I would not have to go where you were leading me. I chatted to pass the time. It was so pleasant to chat. I made patterns with your books on the floor, and thought of riddles and puzzles, to beat you at. You were not quick at those. There was a Mr Ingleton, who used to telephone you about his son. Wanting an appointment at the hospital. What was he like, and what of Mrs Ingleton? You thought, perhaps she was rather grim. I did not like that man ringing you up. Did you see him today? You told me not to be so silly, but I went on and on, until he went abroad.

Your secretary came on Tuesdays for dictation. I did not like her coming or hearing her busy footsteps on the stairs. You asked me to leave before she arrived so as to avoid a confrontation at the door. I said: 'No.' I would like an introduction, and perhaps we could become friends. Have lunches together and all that. You said that you did not think it would be possible. When you went to the door to let her in, I got inside the knee-hole of your desk. I curled myself up so small that it hurt. You would not be able to see me. What pleasure it gave me when you could not find me. You did not know what to do with your secretary. She had to wait in the next room, blushing and bursting with embarrassment. It took some time for you to find me. It was a test on your dignity and on your nerves. When you discovered me, you were very clever. You managed not to laugh and turned things round and made me feel the fool. It was getting later and later, and the secretary was still waiting in the other room. I went further and further, and pushed you too far. I knew what I was doing. It was a question of time. I decided to make the time go wrong, and destroy it. I lay down under your piano. I held on to one of the big brown legs.

'You can't get me out. I won't move. What will you do about it?'

You said that you would call the police.

The police. You would not turn me to the police, but you had said it. You became the enemy, and the spiky rain from outside fell on me. I was terrified, not of the police, but of you. I cried all the way on the bus, and throughout the evening. I had tortured you, and you had shown that you could be merciless too.

Dr Frey says that I am living in the present. Other people would say that I was living in the past. I do not always pay attention to what other people say, and Dr Frey is sometimes difficult to understand.

I do not know anything, except for the fact that I must write to you; for you are now, and will be for ever, my present. I am not satisfied. My hunger is too great. You told me that I was greedy. It is a terrible fault and sin of mine, and the trouble of the whole world. Yearn. That is a word of such strength it makes me afraid, but only it will fit my longing for a present outer reality of you, and of loving.

Last night in Zürich I heard some music. Sentimental, nostalgic dance music, but not without quality. Like a waltz which is not strictly in three-time, and one, therefore, which you do not forget. I was sitting with you at a table in a café. I think that you were wearing your hat. We were listening to the music together. We were not talking. You were on a visit here. It was a delight. Then the music came to an end, and I found myself in my bed in the hotel. What an intolerable pain it gave me to find that neither the café nor the table was there, and that I could not lean over and touch your arm, or smile at you again. (I did not smile at you so very often, after all.) How can that be living in the present?

Of course, when I was with you, a great deal of time was taken up by the past and the future. You only allowed me the present occasionally. Sometimes, though, you would forget allowances and rules, and we would be in the present together, like eternity.

Easter was coming. I began to fear the holidays increasingly. Like Christmas, I loved Easter once. We picked cowslips and primroses to decorate the screen in the church at home, and I would wait for mid-day on Good Friday for the sky to darken. I know that was what Nan said, but she happened to be right. It always does, whatever the calendar may say. Saturday was a day of limbo and of waiting, with the altar still covered in its purple cloth. On Sunday I would wake up and see the sun and the blue sky, and I would shout out loud in my room: 'Christ is risen.' The life of the Christian year will not come through to me now as it used to. Maybe it will again in a different way. I have been troubled all my life; but I did not talk to you about religion then.

You were going to the west country, and I was going to Scotland, with Larissa and Colette and my cat. I was more anxious about leaving you than last time. Supposing you did not come back, and I would never be in your room again? Separation was an agony for me which, as soon as one holiday ended, started again in anticipation of the next. Your grey Rover car was parked in the road. It was old and solid. You had driven me in it once, when I was not well enough to get back. You were a fast driver. Sometimes when no one was looking I inspected the tyres, to make sure that they were not wearing thin. You told me that you were careful about such matters. You knew how vital it was to take care of yourself as best you could, and not die. You did not mind about dying, yourself. I really do not think that you did. You were not preoccupied with death.

I gave you the miniature of my mother before you went away. It is an oval shape and has a blue enamel frame. It is beautiful. It was painted when she was three. She wears an amethyst locket round her neck, and in her hands she holds pink roses. On the gold back of the miniature, in the centre, under glass, some of her hair is twined; it is very fair. She died on her birthday when she was thirty-three, and I was three. Every year my father would take my sister and myself to her grave on April 1st. We took flowers to lay upon it. He asked me to promise always to do so, when he was no longer here. But I could not make myself go there alone. I had not the courage. You told me not to worry for that year. You said it would be good to do something different for once, and you put the picture of my mother in your wallet in the breast pocket of your coat. You kept it, and took it with you on your journeys away. As I write this, the picture of my mother lies in your room, in the drawer of your desk.

I wrote this for my father, and it also still lies in the drawer of your desk.

> We stood at her grave side
> Soft sand stone hard red rock.
>
> Winter passed when we came on
> Her birth day her death day.
>
> Lilies for your wedding
> Let them last let them stay.
>
> Take the tears which I'm shedding
> You could not you did not.
>
> I promise I will come
> When you are dead and gone.
>
> Now that you and love are lost
> I cannot and have not.

*

For a few days the country round my house in Scotland looked more beautiful than I had ever seen it. It was like early summer. Spring was coming too fast. For once the wind did not snap the fat heads of the crocus. The sky and the sea and the loch were blue, but the small wading birds were still in their white winter plumage. The bulbs, which I had planted in the autumn, appeared. There were the wild daffodils on the bank. They call them Lent lilies. When they have been there for many years,

41

their flowers open green. It interests me to put a vase of wild green daffodils in a bedroom for someone. They are so very pretty, but they appear to make the person ill at ease. The cream and white narcissi were opening too, and they do not usually flower until May. They are the hybrids of triandrus; Thalia and Tresamble. Dozens of plants arrived from nursery gardens in pots and boxes, all wrapped in straw. I write down some of them because I miss hearing their names : saxifrage fortunei and alchemilla mollis; hebe and crambe cordifolia; salvia turkestanica and ballota; geranium phaeum and thyme; phlox, Mother of Pearl, and the rose, Reine des Violettes, and a climbing rose with a name like Dittersdorf. I wish I could remember it.

I left Larissa and Colette by the loch at Little Ferry while I planted. My cat came out in the warmth and sunned herself on the branch of the walnut tree. She was still aloof, but always so sprightly there. She was such an aristocratic cat, except for her tooth. It had happened when she was a kitten, and Martin had been playing bean-bag for her, swinging it round and round. She caught the bean-bag in her mouth and it pulled her tooth. It stuck out sideways and never went back again. She was a brave little cat, and I loved her.

You wrote so kindly to me, and telephoned from your village twice. I wrote you too, but for a very few moments I had been seduced by that country. It gave me a strength of its own. I had often noticed it. There are one or two days of restlessness when I first arrive; and then I find slowly that I am held, but by what I do not know.

You knew it did not last that time. My stepmother and her mother came to stay, and we all got on agreeably. They went to lunch with friends, but I could not make myself go. I found running the house a strain, but I made it as perfect as I could.

The wild beaches. How I love their desolation, and their cold. But I was unhappy without you. I have not been back since. You knew the worry and responsibility of it made me sick, and that I was too afraid to go there. My thoughts go round and round. Always the same. They end, wondering whether the saxifrage fortunei has grown.

•

I reached you again. Your room was still there, and so were you. What a relief it was to me. No one appreciates enough what you have, while they have it. Only when it is gone do they realize what they had. I have moaned to you, and have apologized to you for my moaning. Needlessly. Although I did not tell you, I half-knew what I had. This time. Amongst the rubble of my insignificant life, I had found a jewel-stone, so valuable that no other, in all the universes of the empyrean, could replace it.

That is all. I shall not search any further. It is of no avail, for no other exists.

Dr Frey says that he believes the dead turn away when they die. I think I know what he means; and so did you. As always I ask of you, too much . . .

Turn back for a moment, to arouse me.

I do not write to you, like some poor women, who perhaps after their most beloved has died, have to be pitied for their derangements or their stubborn sentimentalities. Men too. They are not to be envied for their delusion? No.

Dead though you are, I write to you with a strong clear mind, and I shall continue as you would wish me to, with faith not clouded by anything, until what has to be written is, and comes to rest.

I have not been very well. I am not particularly well. Dr Frey has said that I could return to the Klinik. It is kind of him. I am not going to, though. I no longer find the silent companionship which I used to find there; and if I did, it would impede me.

I must just pause for a while because in writing to you my heart is not strong enough, always. I have written down part of a poem by Edward Thomas, for you. When I first gave it to you, you said after reading it: 'He knew.' (Although you did not approve of his action.) So I give part of it to you again. During my last months with you, I wept each time I heard the words, and I heard them in my head every day. They are not for me though. They are for you. You are now allowed them.

> I have come to the borders of sleep,
> The unfathomable deep
> Forest where all must lose

Their way, however straight,
Or winding, soon or late;
They cannot choose.

Here love ends –
Despair, ambition ends:
All pleasure and all trouble,
Although most sweet or bitter,
Here ends in sleep that is sweeter
Than tasks most noble.

There is not any book
Or face of dearest look
That I would not turn from now
To go into the unknown
I must enter, and leave, alone,
I know not how.

The fall forest towers;
Its cloudy foliage lowers
Ahead, shelf above shelf;
Its silence I hear and obey
That I may lose my way
And myself.*

❀

I do not seem able to rest, so I have written about my tree which
you knew of. I have wanted to be able to write about it for a
long time, but I could not. Although it is nothing, and I wish
something more could be made of this nothing, I am still glad.

Where is that stunted tree I came upon?
On the snowy sìthean in the barren hills,
Nothing did it bear; but a bridal veil
Over its stark arms was lightly laid.
Could it have borne a coronet, a crown,
A tiara tinselled with crystals
In such ether air, for the bride? I think
There was one, tilted amongst the birch twigs.

* 'Lights Out'.

44

I walked through darkness before I found it,
Across the petrified moor. And then was
The tree, with the bride, with me, wholly one.
Now I thirst for the bride, the tree, to be
Once more.

Klinik Waldhaus,
Zürich

I have fallen back again. I have returned to the Klinik. I hoped
that in writing to you I could raise myself out of my bed, out
of the straps which hold me, out of the Klinik, away from
Zürich, back to England, and also away from Dr Frey. It is not
to be. I cannot break the straps, and Dr Frey will not tell me
when I can go.

There are days and nights when I feel that devils possess me,
and I have become so bad that I scream myself into fits and no
longer know what I am doing. A Swiss woman has left the
Klinik because she could not stand the noise, and an Italian girl
has been moved from the room because she thought that I had
a revolver in my cupboard. I am sorry, but I am beyond caring,
so desperate I am. I wish to scream myself to death, or to be
sent away from the Klinik where I do not choose to be. You
told me that I would be like that if I allowed myself, and that
there would be no limit to my fury. You always wanted it, didn't
you, and I would never oblige. Dr Frey says that he might send
me to Burghhölzli, the mental asylum. I know it would be bad
there, but I do not mind. I would get away from Dr Frey who
holds me in a trap from which there is no escape. I cannot get
out of bed or out of the window. I have no money or passport,
neither can I use the telephone, and even a lawyer would not
help me. If I did scream my way out to Burghölzli, Dr Frey says
that he would get me back again after a time.

Nothing ever again will be the same without you. My heart
cannot stand your absence, that is why I wish to die. Must I
fear for it to be bruised even more, however slightly, by someone
else?

I will not give in however hard they try to hold me, or much
like hell the days and nights become. In a moment of exhaustion
I have dreamt of you. For the first time since you died I dreamt
that you were there. You were so physically close to me. You
drew the anguish from me, and told me to live and listen. I will
continue to write to you as I said I would. It is harder than
before; the pain, the loneliness, and the homesickness are more

46

intense. I do not know why. Perhaps it is because my freedom has been taken from me. You came to me, though, you have not deserted me, and that is all I now ask.

Today is Good Friday, and I believe that Jesus Christ is bearing the sins of the world, up to the top of the hill, where they imagined He died.

They think that I have acquiesced to their therapeutic treatment, but never, never, never . . . They cannot know. I say again that I write to you with a strong clear mind, and although it is so difficult I shall try to do so, as you would wish, with a faith not clouded by anything.

> I have a book of pearl.
> Mother of pearl it's made of
> And watered silk; and gold
> Leaf tints each page faultlessly.
>
> I have a book of steel.
> Silver and rubies adorn it;
> And velvet too. Both are
> Carefully held; and guardedly.

They are gilded to perfection with the words Christ spoke on the cross in the darkest of all hours. Those words are imprisoned here. May they be written in the dust of the streets and in the sand on the shores of the earth, for it to keep. The words of the darkest of all hours.

> I'll throw away the pearls.
> Let the waters close over
> The jewels, which are locked and
> Frozen in my encasement.
>
> Can the wind come one day
> To a far hill to free me?
> And may the reeds in the
> Rivers bow to Him in praise.

It is now Easter day, but the Easter I write of was over, and I was once more back with you. It was not like spring. It was cold and wet, and there were still no buds on the trees. You do not notice the season though, in your part of London. There are

47

no trees or grass, only great buildings of red brick, and dirty newspapers lie in the streets. Every day we used to sigh and say, 'Spring never comes to Bishops Road.' Then we would laugh until we felt quite weak, from laughter and the lack of spring.

You had your plants, though : the sweet-smelling geranium and the peculiar plant whose name we did not know. It had been badly treated. I had tried to destroy it many times. I had thrown it crashing to the ground, scattering the earth all over your carpet. I always tidied the mess I made, but I knew that you were agitated. I broke the plant so that only a tiny shoot remained. I cried when I thought that I had killed it, but gradually it began to grow again, not upwards as before, but sideways. I continued to try to kill it, but it grew persistently. It was an enormous relief. You had a small palm-tree in a blue and white pot. It stood on your piano. Overnight it bore the most extraordinary things. They were not blooms or plumes, or flowers, or buds. You could only say that they were things. Comical things. They were a creamy-white colour, and I had never seen the like before. I minded very much about that plant. You said that it did not care that it was not pretty and like other plants. It was something on its own, in its own right and had its own place and value, however it might be. You said I was like that plant, and it gave me such joy and excitement to think I could be it, and that you could love me secretly even though I were not a rose or a lily. Just a dull little palm-tree, in a blue and white pot, shooting out funny creamy-white things of which it was not ashamed. In fact it seemed to feel the opposite, so flamboyantly it showed them. You paid great attention to your plants and got annoyed with the woman in the flat next door, who forgot to water them when you went away.

I hear this as I write, so I will put it down.

> The maidens came
> When I was in my mother's bower;
> I had all that I would.
> The bailey beareth the bell away;
> The lily, the rose, the rose I lay.

The silver is white, red is the gold;
The robes they lay in fold.
The bailey beareth the bell away;
The lily, the rose, the rose I lay.

And through the glass window shines the sun.
How should I love, and I so young?
The bailey beareth the bell away;
The lily, the rose, the rose I lay.

Anon.

*

It is really an effort for me to write of facts and actions, but I suppose to make a completed whole they cannot be entirely left out. I have been shirking from describing what follows. It just does not interest me. I will, however, try to make the most of a very bad job.

I do not think I could have lived through the days of the summer without you. You interviewed my solicitor to make things easier for me. We both disliked him. An old Etonian with a clever brain for winning difficult divorce cases for his clients. There was nothing to win or lose between Martin and me. He did make difficulties by writing me hostile notes and refusing to sign papers. He wanted to see you again. He did not seem to understand why we should be divorced, even though he was living with someone else. He wanted a hearing, and perhaps make you persuade me to drop the whole thing. I wanted you to see him. I wanted him to have every chance possible. I did not wish to divorce him, but what else was there to be done? You did not have a very good opinion of Martin. You positively disliked him I think. You were reluctant to see him, and only agreed if there was a third person present. We chose Maria. You all met at nine o'clock one evening, and Richard was waiting to drive Maria home. I do not really know what happened or what was said, except that nothing was achieved. Martin saw no reason for change, and ended by shouting at you. You said you were not impressed. It was I who felt sad for Martin.

I had written a letter to Thomas. He had been so involved in my life that I think only his word would have enabled me not to turn back. He replied saying he thought it dangerous to advise people on their lives but he was certain I was doing the right thing. Thomas, who has often told me how much he dreaded divorce, and the hideous dividing of possessions of which he would make no claim; Thomas, a devout Roman Catholic, lapsed since his youth, but with the dogma of the Church inescapably ground into him.

I took his letter with me to the court, of which I was so afraid. You said that you wished to come with me, but thought it would not be suitable. Maria drove me to the court and left me there. I wanted to go alone. I swore on the Bible in a very loud voice. I told the judge that I still loved Martin. The judge did not look very pleased. How negative it was of him. I was given custody of Larissa, and Martin was granted what is called 'reasonable access'. The black gowns and the white wigs meant very little to me. The people who wear them are only trained to see right or wrong. They changed nothing for me.

Martin's father is like the law. He sees only black and white. He was so angry with Martin, who had only told his parents of our separation a short while before, that he crossed him out of his will and refused ever to see him again. You helped me write several letters asking him to be more lenient with Martin, but even I could not persuade him to change his mind, and for some reason he is very fond of me. An old man, sitting brooding in his chair, with all the outdoor pleasures which had made his life, taken from him. He had, though, an obstinate selfishness about him. Martin is a changeling in his family.

I went and sat in a church after the court, until it was time to go to you. Courts were almost an every day occurrence for you, with some child or other to be defended. I wished to have a quarter, no even less, of your wisdom.

Thomas came to see me in the evening. Murderous divorce. We did not talk of it.

The practical difficulties which piled up left me so exhausted that I did not feel fit to cope with much else. You were well aware of this, and you tried to deal with them for me, although they tired you too. The financial problem was the one which drained most energy from me. Of course your fees sounded, and were, astronomical. How could it have been otherwise; the hours and hours I spent with you. We had a professional contract which neither of us wavered from for one moment, although I did often have to implore you for your accounts; you got so behind with them. Usually the reason was the lack of a secretary; but you were never very ordered about business matters. I was much more efficient. You knew that my accountant had a Victorian mind, and did not understand the word psycho-analysis, or why it should cost so much. He had probably never heard of Jung, and a psychiatrist meant the same to him as a charlatan. Of course he could have been right, and he meant the best for me, but he told me that I must 'cut down' and put a time limit on my treatment. I was completely reliant on him. You said how strange it was that people were prepared to buy expensive material objects, but when it came to making an investment in their souls they refused to do so, considering it a monstrous indulgence and a waste of money! You interviewed my accountant for me. He has governed the family affairs for forty years, but now I can no longer address a single word to him, even though he may wish one well. I would have liked to have spied on your interview with him at St Agnes's Hospital. You found him a tragic man. You thought it must hurt him dreadfully to smile, to move his face even. You sweetened him as far as was possible. You talked to my aunts on the telephone. You interviewed one of them who is fascinated by medicine in any form, and she was so won over that she told my other aunt, whose main interest is racing, 'It does not after all cost any more than to keep a horse in training.'

When I told you this it delighted you. You had never heard such a thing before, and you laughed for a whole two guineas' worth. I think you could have gone on for the 'Two Thousand Guineas' – but I must not be silly.

The situation, though, had become out of all proportion for them to accept. It would have been useless to try them too far. We entered into a secret deal. We exchanged papers, lodging them in our banks, saying that I would pay half of what I owed you regularly. The rest at a future date when I was free to do so. Or, in the event of either of our deaths, the money would be paid from my to your estate. The whole business bored us both.

I had so little idea then how meaningful those documents were, and how near they were to becoming a reality. You were so unmaterialistic that you would, if you had been able, have given all for nothing. It was just at that time when the doctors went on strike for more money. I am sure they had good reason, but you told me that they made you ashamed of your profession.

You had always enjoyed the plays of Chekhov, and had been interested in his life when you were younger, and perhaps had more time to read. I see you as a doctor with a mind similar to his.

I will not write any more facts now. I have been in bed for a month, and the overwhelming desire and compulsion to write to you as things happened, in their correct order, makes me very tired. I long to get back to your room. I am outside it when I have to record these exterior events which bear no love or growth. You knew that too, which is why you fought so hard to save me from them.

Travelling to you by bus became the greatest pleasure of my day. I escaped from the house, and Larissa, and Colette, and Miss Selincourt's school. I left them all and entered a different world.

Sometimes I got a seat in the front of the bus where there were no interruptions, and I could sit peacefully and think of you; but more often I had to stand. The buses were hot and dirty. The Park was beautiful with pale green leaves and candles of chestnut flowers. Mothers would be holding their babies or young children on their laps. They sat on the sticky seats. They held them very closely, feeding one another from their proximity. The mothers wore proud faces at the prettiness and perfection that they had produced. I tried to sit in the front of the bus to avoid them. Once or twice I saw a small boy of about seven years old who held such appeal for me that I would have taken his hand, and found that he was my son.

If I was late, I became so anxious that I might miss one single minute of my time with you that I would close my eyes at the red traffic lights, or look around for people who wore wrist watches to see the seconds ticking by as the traffic came to a standstill. Then I would run and run through all the people, and finally up the stairs, until I reached your room. 'I am not late' I would shout and I would hide myself in a corner by your cupboard and refuse to speak to you. 'Exaggerated behaviour' perhaps, but it is only those who have experienced it, who can know what it is.

If I was early I would occasionally get off the bus at the Royal Hotel, and give myself a glass of milk and a chocolate éclair and sit amongst the tourists. I liked to feel that no one knew where I was. I would wash my hands with the liquid scented soap and listen to the canned music in the ladies' lavatory. Vulgar luxury has always appealed to me: the sleek rich Jewish men in Gunter's, when I was six. One day when I arrived there was no reply to your bell. It was like a catastrophe. In one second the whole of my world fell in pieces around me, and I thought that you were dead. But, as you showed me again and again in the end you came up the stairs jingling your keys and apologizing; exhausted by the hospital which had kept you late with petty administrative details. So I would wait by your door, and press my face against the frosted glass window beside it, and see all kinds of prismatic images – the Grand Canyon, Wall Street, and naked men and women bathing in a pool. Sometimes I would listen at your door, trying to hear you play the piano which you did whenever you found time. I used to hear some notes, but never very clearly, and I did not like to ask you to play.

Then I would lie in my chair in your room, protected from everything else, even if I were fighting against you, far away from the outside world which I had grown up to sorrow for, and also to reject.

I always hated the leaving. Two hours. 'We must cut it down to an hour and a half,' you said. Why was I always crying? I never wanted to go back alone in the bus. 'I think you will come with me today,' I would say. You were always so patient and waited by the door while I took as long as I could. You only once lost your temper. I know that you nearly hit me, just checking your arm in time. I understood but was afraid and rang your bell to make sure that things were all right.

The buses were very empty at that hour. Seven or eight o'clock. There were couples sitting together, dressed up, going for a spree. I longed to be one of them. I would pass the restaurants where Martin and I used to have dinner together. They would just be opening up. It seemed that every evening I leaned my head against the dusty windows of the buses, and wept and wept.

I had supper with you in your kitchen, in my private world, with just you and your wife. It was a quiet family meal.

*

I dislike the cult of dreams. They should be secret things, and people who are always telling you of what they have dreamt irritate me. Nor do I like hearing psychological discussions between those who do not really know what they are talking about. There is something soft and messy about such people. But I will allow myself to tell you again of the dream concerning my father.

I loved my father so much, but it was always like loving someone who is in the other room, where you cannot reach them. I feared him too, but I have written about that in my diaries. I did not know it but I loved him physically. I longed to caress the back of his neck, and to hold his strong, beautifully kept hands which were so delicately formed. I liked to feel his body against mine when we danced. We used to dance together. He was the only man I really enjoyed dancing with or wished to sit next to at a dinner-party.

One day Martin was sent to stay with us. We had never met him before. He came for a dance in the country. I fell in love with him before I met him, if that is possible. I fell in love with him after reading his book about a German prison camp which he had written with Gerard. As I expected, my father did not like Martin. At the ball I asked my father to dance. I wanted to dance with him more than anyone there. I was wearing a ruby locket which had belonged to my mother. I danced with my father for a long time. He held me very firmly and everything about him smelled sweet. Not long ago, and it is sixteen years since my father died, my stepmother told me what jealousy she had felt then : how she had hated me for taking my father away from her. She had seen the pleasure on his face when I had invited him to dance. Perhaps it was brazen and brash of me. My sister would never have done such a thing.

The dream I told you of . . . I was wearing a scarlet dress, long to the ground, and I was running as fast as I could over the hill to the shore of Loch Buidhe where I was to meet and dance with my father.

How I love to dance. How much I have wept for my father since he died, although I half-wished that he would, so strict he was.

I have once been allowed out of my body, and have been united with him in God. To look at the useless empty shell of your body lying below you; that is liberation. I do not dare to hope to be granted that again. It would be asking too much.

You made me weep for my father once more. How different you were to him. And, although I had not realized it with him, I knew fully how passionately I loved you. It is surely presumptuous to say that with you it was beyond human bounds.

How can I describe your face? It is ridiculous for me to try. I can only build a kind of identikit which has no life at all. Thomas Mann said: 'language can but extol, not reproduce, the beauties of the senses'. I cannot even extol, I can only write a few words of description which convey no picture at all. Short frail build, pale skin, a straight nose broad at the nostrils, thick white hair at sides and back, and a thin mouth which expressed severity, determination and humour. You had ears of the kind I had never seen before. They lay flat against your head, and they were ears without lobes. They gave an unusual and rather odd quality to your head which, although small, had a powerful and dome-shaped structure. The peculiarity of your ears gave one expectations of magic. You thoroughly disapproved of magic, at least you said so to me because you knew that I loved it. Your face was lined and furrowed, but your skin was soft. You were sixty then. Try as I may, I fail at this moment to see you as you must have looked when young. Your hands were not striking. They were just ordinary hands, worn and very clean. How well I grew to know your hands. Your eyebrows were thick and hung low over your eyelids, and your eyes themselves were those of a much younger man, they were so clear and bright. They were a greenish-brown colour, but again I am unable to describe them. They were capable of expressing so many emotions which now elude me. But I remember the time when your face was close to mine, and in your eyes I saw such intensity and compassion that I know I will never see again in anyone. I do not think you were aware of the force they held, or if I knew of the feeling behind them. The moment remains with me, as few impressions that my life can hold.

*

I had told you long before that Thomas's daughter was called Patricia. I wanted very much to know the name of your daughter, but I could never bring myself to ask you. I always looked at the photograph of her and your wife, which stood on the chimney-piece. It had been taken when your daughter was small. Sometimes I wished to tear up that picture. You did not have your photographs in frames.

One day I asked you without hesitating what your daughter's name was. 'Patricia,' you said. I do not think that you really wanted to tell me. I asked you where she went to school. You told me. It was the same school as the other Patricia went to.

I felt more depressed than usual when I caught the bus that night. I had only been back in the house for a few minutes when Colette came and said that there was someone to see me. I did not feel like seeing anyone. Before I could ask her to say I was out, I heard Thomas's voice. I did not think that he would come again so soon, and he had never before arrived without telephoning. He had just called to see if I were all right. I was grateful to him but I failed to cope with the situation. I shook. My hands would not stop trembling and my eyes were red with crying. We talked about Larissa, and of his daughter Patricia. Then he had to leave, so that he could give Patricia her supper. He asked if he might return later, and suggested that we did something together the next day, as it was a week-end.

He telephoned very much later, and said that Patricia seemed to have no inclination to go to bed, and she had persuaded him to drive her to the country the following day. I should have been able to have borne the disappointment. I should have become accustomed, but the pain which I know so well returned to me with such sharpness that I telephoned you. You said if I felt it strongly enough I was to telephone Thomas and thank him for coming to see me, and that I hoped he would have a good day with Patricia, and we would meet again soon. I did this. I know I made it seem like the message of a child, and he sounded annoyed and abrupt. The tone of his voice drove me to what was a frenzy of fear, and I telephoned him again and asked if he were angry? I knew then that once more I had broken our relationship.

You guided me through the week-end, but you said you thought I could do nothing more for months. I knew that your Patricia did not live with you, but oh – I could not bear the thought of either of them.

I dreaded the week-ends. I was afraid to go away. It would have been difficult to leave Larissa, but that was not the reason why I did not go. I took amphetamines to help me through the week-ends. How undisciplined it sounds but I had to make myself high so that I would behave as I should. I cooked and did the shopping and all the domestic things. I was full of energy and made plans for Larissa and Colette, taking them on expeditions. I drank too much in the evenings, and did not wait with so great an anxiety for your telephone calls. Occasionally I would go out to supper with Maria and Richard, but I never went anywhere else.

In spite of the amphetamines I always wore my grey skirt at week-ends. My grey skirt has the utmost importance for me. I always wear it when I am depressed. It is the wrong length to be fashionable, being neither long nor short. It is very old and has concertina pleats like some lampshades. It is made of a smooth worsted terylene, and is a dead and dour grey colour. Martin always hated it. It is part of me. I have had it patched and mended many times. I have a fear of being caught wearing it by anyone who rates the elegance of the moment highly. They would despise it. I told you about my grey skirt and you wanted to see it but I could not make myself wear it in front of you. I had always to wear my nicest clothes when I was with you. You grew so tired of what you called my idealization of you. You persisted in calling it that until I wore you down, and you accepted that that was how it was going to be. I disliked feeling my clothes all crumpled when I rose from my chair, so every day I made a great performance. I took off my skirt and folded it neatly on your piano-stool. Then you put my rug over me. In winter the rug was a thick tartan one, and in summer you spread a covering of a kind of bleached batiste over me. You took off my shoes and put them on again for me at the end. It all took very long but you rarely grew exasperated.

I dislike clothes. I detest their encumbrance, but I pay great attention to them. You wore neat suits, made from small-patterned stuffs, for meetings and the hospital. I got to know your moods by which tie you wore. When you were not working you wore brown or grey trousers and an old maroon-coloured jersey, or a light woollen shirt with an orange woollen tie, loose at the neck. I would not allow you to wear your spectacles. They had heavy black rims, and they changed your face. You never wore them when you were with me except for the times when you had to write out a note or a prescription. You wore metal clips round your arms to keep up your shirt sleeves. When you took off your coat I made you remove the clips. They looked sinister and mechanical and did not suit you. In hot weather you would throw off your coat, tear off your tie and open the neck of your shirt, asking my permission. In heat-waves you wore sandals without socks. I did not like it. My father would not have liked it. You would not give up wearing your sandals. You said that you were not going to be tyrannized by me.

One week-end I took Larissa and Colette to Green Park and to the swings and slides by St James's. Larissa liked the swings and slides but all the way she whined and cried and we had to drag her along. We walked by the Queen's Gallery at Bucking-ham Palace. There was the exhibition of Leonardo da Vinci's drawings. I could not resist the temptation to go in, in spite of Larissa. I have never been so excited by an exhibition. The drawings of the waves, the hair, the water, the blackberries and the minute flowers of the Star of Bethlehem. The whirling roots, the sylph, the sketches for Leda, the group of trees, the deluge drawings with their force and destruction, and the immature lily. Out of all the art treasures of the world I would choose a Leonardo drawing. I became nearly euphoric at the sight of them but Larissa ruined it. I hated her unreasonably. She lay on the floor and we had to leave and she screamed on the way back for a taxi. The three of us were in despair.

The next day I went to you wearing my grey skirt. I brought with me the postcards of Leonardo's drawings, and made an arrangement of them on the top of your bookshelves. You liked my grey skirt and my arrangement. You loved Leonardo. You understood about Larissa and the domesticity. I had made my arrangement on your bookshelves in defiance. I had come to you wearing my grey skirt in shame.

You said that if my face had been lined and old, you would not have loved me the less. What peace it brought me to know that for you love did not depend on an outward aspect of oneself. I ceased to try to hide the perpendicular line on my forehead which deepened when I cried.

I went to see a play by Pinter. There were just two characters on the stage. The woman sits on a chair wearing a skirt exactly like mine. Surely my grey skirt must have a chance at last?

During hot weather you would struggle to open your window. It was made to close as tightly as possible because of the draughts in winter, which pierced through the cracks of the top of the old building, and gave you pains in your back. As soon as the window was opened the noise of the traffic and the jet aircraft, which you detested, would drown our voices and you would have to close it again. You would pull the curtain across to shield me from the sun, and turn on a small electric fan to cool the stifling air. It was one of the days when I knew that you were overtired. The dust and the fumes – the grind of the day with the pressures of the hospital whose rigid authorities you continually seemed to be fighting. I was glad that you would soon be getting a rest, and the peace of the country which you needed so much. But my own pressures were beating me, and the parting from you was drawing near.

In the flat below a very young baby was crying. I cannot stand the crying of a young baby. It seems to express the whole sorrow of life.

I picked the baby up and held it in my arms. My breasts felt nothing, as though they were lumps of stone, but when I held my baby close to me they poured out the milk which is restricted in them, longing always to be freed. I felt my baby's furry head and its little legs like clothes-pegs. It was ecstasy as I held it to me. Then suddenly it was gone. I found I was holding only the rose-coloured cushion which I used to clasp to my stomach when the pain was too great. At the realization, my anger and disappointment were so strong that for a moment everything went black. I put out my hand and seized the first book I could grasp from your bookshelves. I tore the binding from it. I broke its back and then tore the pages again and again. When it was over I wept at what I had done, and you gave me some valium. I stared at the pieces of the book scattered in front of me. It was called *The Nursing Couple*. You said : 'You would have chosen that one,' and confessed you were upset. The book was a first edition, and had been given to you by the author. Its subject was the basis of your whole work.

I took the pieces back with me, and sat up most of the night trying to stick them together. It was an impossible task and the book was never the same again. You said it did not matter and that I was more important. I spent many hours telephoning medical book shops, shops which sold secondhand books, and putting advertisements in columns of newspapers and literary magazines for wanted or out of print books. I contacted the warehouse of Hamish Hamilton Medical Books. *The Nursing Couple* by Merell P. Middlemore, M.D. First published April, 1941. I combed all the likely places in Oxford and Cambridge. For months and months no copy could be found. No one could replace what I had destroyed. Until it was too late.

There have been two separate incidents today. Totally unconnected but because of them I do not know how I have the strength to write. Yesterday I had a letter from Miss Lane from the Clinic in North London. I quote from it. 'Thank you for suggesting that I write to Dr Frey. I should like to do this and then perhaps we should discuss the pros and cons of your seeing

Larissa again. I have written to her foster-parents and asked them what they feel about this because they are the people who know Larissa most intimately now.'

This morning in my dreams I heard the bells tolling and tolling for my dead child. I woke up weeping so loudly that Dr von Eschenbach came to see me. Why under God's laws could it have not been you? There, I catch myself saying it again. 'Just once!' It whispers to me. For how long will the dread of that dream last?

*

You were quite fond of your block of flats although you were always cursing the leaking roof by your front door, the peeling paint on the stairs, and the whole crumbling Victorian structure. The inside of your flat: I think you loved it. It was your home, and your marriage was a happy one. You said anyone who had a happy marriage was fortunate, and you would never do anything that would harm your own.

I am certain, though, it was your essence alone which had made your flat how it was, built up around your life and personality, projecting many years of your work. Your flat had little decoration. It was drab although the sun shone through the window of your room. The walls and carpets had no colour, and the curtains were made of functional cloth, just hanging. You had one or two pieces of furniture which looked as though they had belonged to your family. You had few possessions but what you had was used and cared for. You appreciated and loved beautiful things but you had not the means or I think the desire to own them. You had your books, and your brown grand piano with piles of music on the top, your pictures which you had painted yourself, and two large abstract paintings signed with your initials. I thought that you had painted them, but no – it amused you to tell how you had bought them from a friend, who was an artist, with the same initials. You said that they were real paintings, which you did not consider your own to be. At the end of the long passage there was a small table with a marble top of many colours. It usually had a vase of flowers, sometimes wild ones, upon it. By the heavy front door there was an old engraving of Taynton Park in the west country; by the door of your room some discoloured photographs of your relations, and in the corner a lamp on a stand. It was a large lamp with a narrow shade over three feet high. It was ugly, like a monstrous toadstool. I never liked to look at it but I did not tell you so. When I grew more confident I sometimes asked to go to your bathroom, to wash my hands, to go to the lavatory, and once or twice to be sick. Everything there was clean but it was poor. The wash-basin was cracked and stuck together with sticking plaster. A hot water-bottle hung on a hook, and various medicinal things, not those of young people, lay around. Two dressing-gowns hung on the door. In some foolish way they disturbed me, and I wished to wrap myself in them. Yours was an old plaid one.

Many people I have known, including myself, have been so preoccupied with decorating their homes. Fashionable colours, William Morris wallpaper, pictures and often unread books to fill the empty spaces. Holland blinds with tassels, French headings on the curtains, Victoriana as a trend, or valuable objets d'art. Sometimes the whole is a pretty or an interesting or occasionally beautiful interior, but never ever do the rooms sacrifice themselves to the daily labours of their owners.

A home to be lived in as a refuge from outside but also to support a life's work so serious that no time can be given for vanities to impress others. That was yours.

I loved your flat so much that it is impossible for me to think of it without weeping. Everyone who entered it would have found it pleasant and peaceful, but for all your humour and enjoyment of the senses it portrayed your basic character which was one of suffering and attending to the poor world. Do not laugh at me for using big words. You were suspicious of them, I know.

Outside troubles were mounting for me as the summer progressed. They bore down on me and occupied my thoughts to such a degree that we accomplished little, if any, work together.

I still used to go to the Clinic in North London once a week to see Miss Lane the social worker, and Larissa still went every day. I liked Miss Lane but the more determined she was to weld Larissa and me together, the more determined I became to sever our fake mother and child relationship.

Through all the weeks, the summer holidays were threatening. Colette was returning to France. But I took it for granted that I would take Larissa to Scotland with my cat. You said why did I not do something different and break the pattern of my routine. I had not considered such a thing to be possible. You knew how much I loved my house in Scotland, but after the Easter holidays I dreaded the experience again. There was the loneliness, and the demands of running a house and of keeping up the outward appearance which was expected of me. That, together with the knowledge of your holiday, amounted to such a nightmare for me that I took more and more pills and drank increasingly.

Maria and Richard invited me to stay in Italy in August. I was afraid to accept but you urged me to go. You thought I should have a holiday away from Larissa. You said that it would not hurt her to go to a suitable family for a month. She was too young to be sent to a children's holiday camp, so I went to an agency and found a list of foster-parents who took children to stay in their houses in the country. I chose a family in Somerset. I made careful investigations, and I invited the foster-mother's sister to tea. Larissa and I liked her.

Larissa was continually being asked to parties by her school friends. Coloured invitations would arrive or mothers, unknown to me, telephoned. I dressed her in pretty frocks and fine white socks and black patent leather shoes. She was happy and pleased with herself. I made her take beautifully wrapped birthday presents to the anonymous children. I knew that I should ask them back but the thought terrified me. I bought Larissa a doll's cot decorated with white muslin for her fourth birthday. It did not arrive in time. She, Colette and I had birthday tea in the kitchen. Larissa had asked for a chocolate cake with her name written on it. We sat solemnly, surrounded by crackers and ice-cream. Larissa was good and asked no questions as to why there were no guests. Never had I felt such a failure to her. I feared those robust mothers with their balloons and conjurors, their egg and spoon races and ingenious games; the nannies separate in a bunch; the cocktails at the end for the occasional father who came to collect his children. Colette fetched Larissa in taxis. I would have liked to have been included but what is the use of wanting to fit into a mould when you have proved that you definitely do not? I wished happiness for Larissa. For a child, a large part of happiness means to be like other children. I never had a birthday party either, but why should she suffer the same? When I was older I went for mysterious birthday expeditions with my father in Scotland, planned to the last detail by me. Perhaps Larissa will one day find the same, and learn that it is not essential to conform? She was so young though, and I could give her no love. Three times during those weeks I had to quickly leave the room before I hit her. One day she clutched at me and I screamed at her to go away because I could not bear her touching me. I cannot forgive myself for that. I am her, and she is me, and I do not want her. We are too painful to each other.

One night, you tried to telephone me but you got no answer. There was a fault on the line but it worried you, and you came to my house and rang the bell. Neither Colette nor I answered the doorbell at night. It was half-past ten and I was getting into bed. I leaned out of the window and saw you standing there. I had always wanted you to put me into my bed. Every night when you telephoned, I longed for your bodily presence. I could not believe you had taken the trouble to come, or that I was not dreaming. My cat was asleep on my eiderdown. You had never seen her. You did not dare touch her in case you woke her up. You put me into my bed, knowing how delighted I was, and wrapped the clothes around me. 'Just for this once,' you said, with a note of surrender in your voice.

*

Larissa went to Somerset by train. I took her to the station to meet the foster-mother's sister, and said good-bye to them. Larissa was pleased about her holiday and when I spoke to her on the telephone after she had arrived she sounded quite happy. Colette left for France. My cat went to a cat's home not far from

London, where the owner knew her so well that she kept her in her house.

I delayed going to Italy until you went to the west country. For a whole week I felt the absence of the daily domestic routine as a yoke of hatred lifted off me. I was afraid of going to Italy. I was afraid of leaving you, of disasters, of the aeroplane, and of the people I would meet. I had not been with people, collectively, for over two years. I was afraid of catastrophes without you being there, of the feeling that the house was falling down on top of me, and of the spiky rain. The fear of sitting with a stranger or an acquaintance, knowing that I would be unable to produce a leisurely flow of words or even a stilted conversation. The thought terrified me.

I found something to make it better; a joke between us. Something that I could think about, supposing the worst should happen. I had been reading a biography of Ronald Firbank. I came across a description of him in his elaborately decorated rooms at Oxford. The Sitwell brothers had called on him. When one of them complimented him on his novel, *Caprice*, Ronald Firbank could not cope with the situation. He must have felt the suspense, the desperate but failed attempt at contact between people, the silence, and the presence of the objects in the room staring him in the face. The tension must have been too much. Firbank turned his head away and remarked in a choking voice, 'I can't bear calceolarias! Can you?'

I had to explain a little before you saw the joke. A calceolaria is a particularly unattractive pot plant, with bright yellow pouch-like flowers (defined in the dictionary as slipper-shaped) spotted in red, brown and orange. Calceolarias and their total unrelatedness to the situation. You saw the point, and we enjoyed it greatly, but I think it was more my brand of humour than yours. However, I was taking the calceolarias to Italy, and they would give me support. I practised the joke on you many times.

For several days I saw the preparations for your departure gathering in the passage. You said that you would visit Larissa on your way. The last day, I would rather not have gone to you. I feared our partings so, though they were always calm and controlled. The training of my father carried me through, as it has carried me through many things. You took the miniature of my mother with you in your wallet and telephoned me from the box down the hill half-an-hour after you arrived.

The calceolarias did not protect me from the people I feared.

Pisa, Lucca, San Gimignano, Volterra. I enjoyed being in Italy and visiting those places again. In Lucca, the square that is not a square is the most perfectly proportioned architecture I have ever seen. I remember coming upon it for the first time with Martin, neither of us knowing of its existence previously, and just staring, both of us mute and unbelieving that such harmony in building could be. The poverty though – it is crumbling away – washing hangs from the windows, small boys kick their footballs and fight, and old crones dressed in black sit at a table in the centre playing bingo.

Villa Brentano, in the country not far from Lucca, was the house Maria's parents had bought that year. There was also a small farmhouse in the olive-grove which was where Maria and Richard's guests stayed, while the villa was used by Sir Max and Lady Calder, and Mary, Muriel, Rosalind and Rachel, and all the other children who came and went. I had a little room in the farmhouse where at night you could hear the ripe pears dropping off the trees and thudding on to the ground between the rows of vines. Small scorpions hid in the beams on the ceiling and mosquitoes bit one to pieces. There were sunny days and rainy days; and one found corners which impressed on one a perfect Tuscan scene.

Maria worked so hard to keep all her friends, her parents and aunt, and the many children happy that I think the strain was great. Drinking-water had to be fetched from a spring every day, and huge picnics for lunch and dinner produced. Pizzas and wine, and pasta and tomato salads. People came and went and visits were made to the area around Sienna, where there were more friends. Sir Max drove to Florence, and the Israeli girl who looked after the children read her Hebrew newspapers without good grace. There were conversations and arguments and chatter and intrigues, and Maria bore the brunt of the generation gaps. Richard had to return to London twice for his work, and I think she missed the lack of his serenity to smooth over and carry things along. There were many enjoyable times. Maria and Richard make things enjoyable for everyone. I stayed there for a month. I took amphetamines every day, more and more until they ceased to have any effect. I knew most of the people who came to stay. I knew them as acquaintances when Martin and I were married. As I write, I see them pass before me in a parade. I list them as a kind of fascination. I like names. I liked the people too; that, in a way, was the trouble. Here they are with their children. Anne and Miles with James. Paul and Carlotta with Frances and Hugo. Henry and Jane with Victor and Benjamin. Antonia and Philip, Charles, Georgina, Juliet, and David and Claire. Jonathan with Isolde, Katherine, Andrew and Louisa. Alastair and William, and those who made visits who lived within range. Peter, Laura, Vivienne and Mark. Josephine with Stephan, Ingrid and Desmond with Elizabeth and Edward; and Maurice and Nigel, two writers, who only came to London during the winter to see their publishers, and to peer in on the social scene. The rest of the year they worked in their well-hidden Tuscan house which was surrounded by a garden filled with lotus flowers, where only favoured friends were invited.

You could lie under an olive-tree reading a book, go on expeditions or play games with the children. That was the scene.

I tried hard to be happy and to speak to them all, or to make some trivial remark to any of them in order to feel I had established some contact. I used to think out what I might say, and then I would act it out, and they would listen like strangers and not truly understand what I meant. Secrets and jokes of which I had no real part, and I knew once again, I proved once more, that their casual social speech was not mine. I would return to my room discouraged and often in despair. I am sure it was my own fault. All of them had their own troubles and sorrows and sometimes I sensed them coming through, but they could behave in a regular cheerful way in conformity with the scene. How I wished to be like them, spontaneous, outwardly normal, gifted in different ways, and able to cope with human harmony in the world. But it was nothing unusual. It was just the same as it had always been.

I had letters from you but I found it hard to answer. I just longed to be with you again, to climb your stairs and to see the number 50 painted in black on the frosted glass window beside your front door. To me, that number 50 was the sign to the gateway into my paradise on earth.

In Italy I received a packet of letters from Martin. They were written with such aggression that they filled me with misery. It did not help. In a curious way I was afraid of all the children. They treated me warily, as though I were not of their parents' friends. They were children who were already growing up to inhabit the other kingdom. I wondered what Larissa was doing, and the children who knew her questioned me closely about her. She had, after all, lived for nearly a year with Maria and Richard and they loved her.

One day, hard as I tried to stop it, everything seemed to collapse around me. Maria helped me. She prevented the house from falling down on top of me, by talking of you. I made myself join a picnic expedition but I felt so sick and shaken that I knew very well I infected some of those present.

Soon after I became physically ill. The pains in my back and stomach were so sharp that I found it hard to walk. I did not wish to tell anyone and I bought some pills in the chemist in Lucca. Richard and I and William, with three of the children, were going to Pisa to meet somebody at the airport. The aeroplane was late, and we went and sat in a café close to the leaning tower. The children wanted to climb it but were not allowed to go alone. It was Richard who should stay with William, a middle-aged visitor, whose reluctance to climb the tower showed understandably on his face. Obviously I was the one to go. It was very hot. I could feel the ground burning beneath my feet. Every step jarred me. I did not know whether I could manage to climb the tower. I do not like climbing the leaning tower of Pisa at any time but this was so agonizing that I shall never forget it. I trod the endless steps very slowly and the children raced ahead of me to the parapet at the top. I clung on to the railings and everything went round and round at that ghastly angle. The heat and the terrifying slant and the pain. The blinding whiteness of the cathedral, and the green far below were swimming together before my eyes. I could not have saved a child from falling. I could not move. I do not know how I got myself and the children down again. The bumping of the car on the way home was almost more than I could bear. The new guest had arrived and I had to appear normal. But I was forced against my will to tell Maria and go to bed. I had a fever and the pain was such that I could not stand upright. The local doctor came. He said that he thought it was a chill on the kidneys. He gave me some pills which were so strong that they killed the pain immediately. As long as I took them every two hours I could keep going. I was leaving the next day. There was no seat on an aeroplane from Pisa so I took the train from Lucca, changing at Florence for Milan. The train was very crowded and I was squeezed between lines of hot Italian men. I managed the journey only because of the Italian doctor's pain killers. I flew from Milan to London, and kept swallowing the pills to keep me from fainting. I arrived at my house in the middle of the night. The house was empty and wonderfully still, and I lay on my bed in a daze and thought of all the people I had encountered. There had been enjoyable times, and I remember thinking vaguely that my heart was alive like all those people. I was not any different but it was as though I had become frozen between two extremes. The longing for normal love which marriage and children can bring; and the intense desire to create a something near to perfection. I do not understand, and I fail and fail. I have no home except with you, and even that – I knew. I was to see you again the following day, and for that moment I was, perhaps, the most fortunate one living.

*

You were there, and you looked well and rested. We did not talk very much for several days. I needed to stay close to you and be very quiet. I did not seem to have much physical strength. I had been to the doctor the day after my return but all he did was to sneer at the Italian pain killers and give me antibiotics. The pain was less but it still hurt to walk. Every day you took my temperature, which you said was not normal. I could not rest. The Clinic in North London was asking when

Larissa was coming back. The time was overdue. Every day I tried to find someone to replace Colette, without success. I also had to find a new driver with a car. I advertised and inquired at agencies for someone to take Larissa to the Clinic each day. A male telephone operator and a retired policeman applied, but I did not think they would be suitable. I went through all the motions of preparing for Larissa's return but I did not tell the foster-parents that I was back.

I had told the owner of the cat's home the date of my return. She telephoned in great distress and said my cat had been missing for three weeks. I knew that was the end of my beloved little cat. Her kitten, whom I loved even more than her, had gone the same way. She had always been waiting for me by the front door when I came back from you, and she played with glass beads so gracefully on the wooden kitchen floor. I did not talk of her or think of her. I froze her in my mind. My small brown cat. My magic cats. I cannot write of them. They have gone.

The objects which I had asked Martin for from the flat began to arrive. There were also the belongings of my past: piles of clothes, letters, theatre programmes, business documents from years back, and hundreds of dusty books. Amongst the entanglement were littered things which Martin had accumulated in his charmed but untidy life. In a moment of stress I saw it as a collage, close to hell, which he had sent me on purpose. I opened an envelope which the removal man handed to me. In it was a book called *How not to Kill your Husband*. Martin had also sent Larissa's baby-basket which she had arrived in when she was ten days old, and her baby-bath and clothes. I gave them to the removal man. I do not know what I would have done if Mrs Watson had not been with me. I could disguise nothing from her. She, too, was unhappy. In retrospect, I see that Martin was so shocked and hurt that I had done what I said, that he was pouring all the darkness of his shadow upon my head. He was hardly aware of it. I was not without guilt, and I would not write these words, which would be best left unwritten, if they had not been the truth of the moment, and therefore part of us.

I went to you that day with the book Martin had sent me,

so that you could throw it away for me. I also took you a photograph of myself which I had found amongst the rubble. I showed it to you because it was the way I felt, and it was the only means I had to express to you my feelings. Martin had taken the photograph the first summer he came to stay in Scotland. It had been June, and we were there alone. In the photograph, I stood at the edge of a loch which was hidden in the hills. I was naked. All over my breast and ribs were deep cuts and wounds. They had been caused by the sword-like leaves of the wild iris, and twigs of the alder wood where we had lain together the night before, surrounded by wet moss and drifts of white garlic flowers, and trees of wild plum. I thought that I had found happiness. So badly in need of comfort I was that I inflicted on you the picture which you could not bear to see.

Martin, my friend and companion. Warily, but for ever part of me. Loving in his own way; if not in mine.

*

Consciously I had been preparing for Larissa's return but suddenly something snapped inside me and I telephoned the Clinic in North London. Miss Lane was not obtainable. The secretary asked me what I wished to speak to her about. I said that Larissa would not be returning to the Clinic because she would no longer be living with me. You had always told me I could reach you at the hospital any time I wished, and that I could get through the barriers of the Department of Child Psychiatry by saying that it was at your request. I repeated to you what I had done, and you told me to leave the matter entirely to you. I expected you to be angry when I saw you that evening. You were not. You had spoken to Miss Lane and had arranged a meeting between her and yourself and another representative of the Clinic. You told me to contact the foster-parents and to ask them if Larissa could stay for a few more weeks. I remember sitting stunned at what I had done. I had dragged myself to you. I could hardly speak or walk. The pain and the fever had returned so you sent me back in a taxi and told me to go to bed.

I telephoned the foster-mother who was practical and unmoved at what I asked her. Larissa was well and seemed to be enjoying life with the other children and their animals, and with the family trips to the sea. The foster-mother had been interested to meet you. You had told me that you had been impressed by the homeliness and goodness of the family. I believe that you had given her an idea of the situation. You had seen that an understanding with her could be a valuable asset, perhaps for other times.

I remained in bed for the next ten days. The doctor said he could find nothing wrong, but I was continually in pain. You talked to him but found him unsympathetic. He was not of your kind. He just thought I was being neurotic. You came to see me every day, and I would throw you the key from my bedroom window. You would let yourself in, and climb the narrow staircase to the top. One evening the pain became so acute I told the doctor that he had to do something. He sent an ambulance, treating it as a joke, and I was taken to the Harley Street Clinic, where I did not want to go. Mr Evans, a gynaecologist, said there was something wrong and that he should operate. The doctor said, no – I was only there under observation. Mr Evans is almost a friend. He had operated on me twice before. He made me new fallopian tubes, sewing in pieces and repairing the damage which is something few surgeons can do. All the others I had seen said, 'Adopt another child, and forget it.' He had not. He made the tubes good, just before Martin and I separated. He works in the Chelsea Hospital for Women, and takes care of the more fortunate ones with their babies in Queen Charlotte's. His consulting rooms are in Harley Street. He dresses for the part a little clownishly because his pin stripe suits and the carnation in his buttonhole do not go with his personality. I believe he wears them because he thinks he ought to. He is a serious joker. That is why you liked each other, the very first time you met. He and the doctor did not agree. Days of pain continued. I told them, perhaps too sharply, that I thought doctors were supposed to cooperate. I began to swell and swell. I felt I was being punished once again. A false pregnancy to mock me. You could do nothing but you helped me by staying with me as much as you could. I asked Mr Evans if I could be moved to the Chelsea Hospital for Women because Harley Street was so far for you to come. He said with regret that it would be against hospital regulations. The doctor was forced to agree and I was operated on. They made me sign the usual paper and I wrote your name as my next of kin. I think you were quite pleased. I said that if I had a cancer, Mr Evans was to promise not to remove anything which would prevent me from having a child, and if necessary was to stitch me up leaving the cancer inside me. You said it would not be fair to him, and would be so against medical ethics it could not be considered. I was not brave, and I cried and cried because it was that which distressed me so. Multiple cysts on both ovaries, and three weeks in the Harley Street Clinic. That was all. Both you and Mr Evans finally convinced me that nothing had been done to harm my reproductive capacity. You came to see me every day. We hated the Harley Street Clinic, with the sound of the traffic roaring as though it were in the room. You did not wish Martin to know where I was. He sent flowers to my house but they died in the empty basement. Like everyone I dread operations and the depression which goes with them. I am afraid I cried every day when you came. I returned to my house with a nurse from New Zealand. I caught an infection and was in bed for another two weeks. Every day you would come, keeping an eye on the nurse, and checking with Mrs Watson, visiting her in her house in Wandsworth Bridge Road. It was difficult to explain your presence to the nurse. Nurses are inclined not to understand. You wanted me back in your room and it was all I wished for.

You had the meeting with Miss Lane and the other representative of the North London Clinic. They were adamant that Larissa should return for treatment, even if it meant moving her to foster-parents in London.

*

Poor Larissa – to hand her to strangers again. It was a cruel thought and you did not agree with it. You told them you could make no progress with me if Larissa and I were living together, and that you wished her to remain where she was for the time being, visiting me as often as possible. You defied the North

London Clinic, with which you had always been so closely linked, and which you had persuaded to take Larissa in the first place. I knew that you did not like going against a board and body of people of your profession. They could not but respect your opinion even though they disagreed with it. But I sensed it made you uncomfortable. Never did I see you lack courage of any kind. The one thing I knew you dreaded for yourself was illness; real grave illness, not like mine. You had seen so much of it. Physical illness dragging on and on. I am thankful you were spared that particular endurance test. Had you not experienced most others? I only guess.

You went away for a few days in November. It was half-term for school children, and a time when the pressure of your work was eased. You went to the west country and visited Larissa on your way. Apart from a few quarrels amongst the children, you found all was well.

I was sent to convalesce with my aunt in the country. She lives alone, and has a farm where she breeds racehorses. It is quiet and peaceful there. She has people to look after her so one does not have to do anything but eat and sleep and read, and go for walks in the large melancholy garden. The garden has been allowed to go wild, with hens and vegetables filling the spaces where herbaceous borders once were.

You had a telephone installed in your house in the west country, so that you could keep in touch with me on your holidays. You had never had one there before. One of your reasons for having a holiday was to escape the telephone which perpetually harassed you in London. I could not understand that you would go to such lengths for me in order to lessen the torture of your absence. Torture, I do assure you, is not too extravagant a word. You rang me nearly every evening with your new telephone. I think you were almost pleased with it. My aunt would take the call while she was feeding the dogs. She did not mind and was never curious, just saying how kind and charming you were.

I started to write again while I was there. I worked on 'Eleanor'. I had put it aside for so long and I knew that I had to finish it. Was I not writing of her and my home to prevent me from dying? I was not sure how much time I had, so I sat for hours at the desk pretending to my aunt that I had many letters to write.

In the autumn garden I came across a clump of St John's Wort. I picked one of the green slightly sticky buds and squeezed it tightly between my finger and thumb. Its powerful and bitter smell, with a touch somewhere of sweetness, came right over me until it transported me back into the garden at home, when I was a child. I do not know for how long I smelled it, but I buried my face in my hand finding the places where its fragrance led me. It was irresistible. When my mother died I convinced myself that one day she would return. Everything I touched and smelled in the garden were hers: the smell of St John's Wort, and the foxy taste of the Crown Imperial, primulas and cowslips, and all the wild flowers. I was happy to live in her domain. There were times when I cannot imagine that anyone could have been happier than me. You, and my home I speak of, are one, because you are my lost paradises. I do not expect others on earth.

As I write, I hear a Beethoven quartet on the wireless that Schwester Trudi has lent me. I stop to look again at your photograph. I listen to the music with you. It gives me the courage to proceed with this miserable day. I have no St John's Wort or any of the other flowers to smell, but Beethoven compresses them all. He compresses everything, not only the fragrances. Who was it who said that Beethoven preached?

I am well. They say I am sick. Am I? I do not feel at all sure. Please envelop me tonight.

You were determined that I should not live alone in my house. You suggested that I should have a lodger or a housekeeper. I did not want a lodger or a housekeeper. I liked the quiet and privacy I had achieved. My solitude, although hard, gave me the freedom to live in an inner world. I made a routine which I knew would be upset by the presence of a stranger. I woke late in the morning which made me guilty and ashamed. I have always been tired and exhausted in the morning, sleeping so deeply that it seems as though I were a level below the ordinary unconsciousness of sleep. When I was fifteen my father used to call me in time for breakfast. He would come to my room while he was shaving and pick me up in his arms and drop me on to the bed. I was bad-tempered and cross at being woken and I thrashed out at him once too often. He told me that he would come no more. I did not believe him, but he never came back. I implored him to change his mind, and wept silently in my room so that no one should hear. But he never returned to me again.

Often you would telephone me in the morning before you left for the hospital to tell me something had occurred to you that could not wait, or to change the hour if you had a meeting which you had forgotten about. A few times I went to you at nine o'clock in the evening. I did not like the time being changed, so rigid a pattern had I set myself in order to keep on the level. I worked in the mornings on 'Eleanor'. I wrote in longhand and rewrote on my typewriter. I became more and more absorbed in it. Eleanor's emotions terrified me, and I could not tell whether anyone would guess what lay behind her mask.

Mrs Watson would arrive at half-past twelve and I would return for a while to inhabit the house where I was supposed to live. We had long discussions and laughed at all kinds of things. She was my companion for one hour every day during the week. I would then go out in to the streets, revelling at the thought that I had no jam or biscuits to buy. I ate tinned soup and a baked-potato for supper, and I lunched late, often at three o'clock, in an Italian café. I sent Larissa postcards signing myself 'Mummy' in the smallest possible letters – I hated the word. The first one I sent her was of a picture of Peter Rabbit. I showed it to you, and although I like Peter Rabbit it seemed so false for me to send it to Larissa that I tore it into pieces. I think you half-agreed with me. The next card I sent was of Tower Bridge.

They got me a lodger, or rather Maria did; a girl who was looking for a job whose presence immediately became a nightmare. The telephone never stopped ringing and she always answered it even if it happened to be for me. She gave dinner-parties and broke things, and strange men were always at the door. She never pulled the curtains back in Larissa's play-room before she went to bed, so it would all be in darkness in the morning. She had breakfast at mid-day with her friends in the kitchen. She was untidy and dirty, and I am afraid I am so incurably fastidious that she drove me mad. I was nervous too. I felt that the house no longer belonged to me, and I hardly dared return to it. She had taken it over with her youth and beauty, her strength, and her gay laughing world. Larissa was coming to stay. I was in a great state about it. I asked the lodger if she could go away for the night so that Larissa and I could be alone. She unwillingly obliged.

Larissa arrived with the foster-parents. I showed them upstairs to the sitting-room. I was certain that Larissa would cling to the foster-mother. To my amazement she came straight to me and sat as close as she could as though she knew it to be her rightful place. She was quiet and beautifully mannered and spoke with a slight west country accent. The foster-mother is a proper mother. She is not pretty, but her lap must be nice for Larissa to sit in. We had tea in the kitchen, and our conversation and discussions of arrangements were as they should have been. Larissa did not mind at all when they left. She did not mention my cat, and neither did I. We talked of her life in Somerset, and of Colette, and of Scotland, and also of you.

'He's mine.'

'No he isn't, he's mine.'

We had quite a good time. I gave her a bath and put her to bed. She slept well that night, and the next morning at six o'clock, before it was light, I woke to hear her opening her chest of drawers. I watched her through the slightly open door. She was going through all her toys and oddments, little bits and pieces, discovering them again, and making certain that everything was still there. She was so intent and busy that she did not notice me, and I left her, thrilled and hectic in her minute world. I did not go to sleep again. I lay listening to her touching, smelling, turning, lifting and pushing, until she had satisfied herself, and had everything in her own particular order.

Oh, Larissa, if ever you should read this – I know, I know, just how important it is, and how I crave for it too – still. Yet what am I doing for you? I am lying in a clinic in Zürich because I am unable to give you the kernel which all human life must have, from which to be able to grow. I cannot continue this now. I feel too sad. I will tomorrow. Before I leave the Klinik I shall try to tell what you, my doctor, were going to do, so that whether I am alive or dead, Larissa might read it, and perhaps understand.

Please will you help me to do what I should do, and surely that for which I was born. Something has grown within me which prevents and refuses it. Or was I made like that? You were beginning to know. How greatly I love you; you who loved Larissa too.

Larissa and I had breakfast rather shyly together in the kitchen. We were definitely making conversation. She had dropped her west country accent and I could hear her copying the intonations of my voice. She was trying so hard. She asked why her toys had been moved from her cupboard in her play-room to her chest of drawers. I explained to her as best as I could, and she seemed satisfied. It was a dark November Sunday, and it was pouring with rain. Larissa spent the morning trying on her new winter clothes. She was extremely pleased with them and spent a long time in front of the looking-glass. I told her Mrs Watson was coming to see her, and that she was going to take her back to the foster-parents. She called them Aunt and Uncle at that time. The family was staying with a relative in Soho and they were to give a party in the afternoon. I had washed all Larissa's clothes the night before and had packed them in her bag, dressing her in her new party frock. She said good-bye quite happily and went off with Mrs Watson who had bought her a toy trumpet. Apparently she blew it all the way in the taxi to Soho, stopping once to say very quietly: 'I wish I could stay with you and Mummy.'

That Sunday afternoon I sat on the sofa until it grew dark, looking out at the rain and the dismal sky. I was glad that Larissa had gone. I had enjoyed her visit. I enjoyed it while she had been there. I had given her love but I knew that I could not have sustained it for another day; the depression it left me with was unbearable. I watched the house opposite. It belonged to a man who I used to know at Oxford, when I was at school there. I often see him coming home from work with his prosperous-looking briefcase but I have never encountered him. Maybe he would not remember me. I watched him and his wife and children having tea in their brightly lit room. I began to share it with them but when the lamps in the street came on they drew their curtains against prying eyes. I sat in the dark for a long time. Larissa would be enjoying herself now in her new frock at the party with her trumpet and all the children and the jellies and ice-cream. I was glad that I was not there.

Mrs Watson told me that after she left Larissa and had returned to her home she had been miserable for the rest of the day. I just sat and did nothing but wait for your telephone call. When the lodger returned I told her I was sorry but I could no longer keep her, and I pretended that Larissa was coming back. I gave her a week to find somewhere else. I tormented myself that I had used Larissa for my own benefit. That night the child next door took to inconsolable crying. You said that under the circumstances you found the lie perfectly excusable, and all word of lodgers or guests was temporarily put aside.

We continued. Sometimes doggedly, which the dictionary says means 'grimly persistent'.

You did not talk to me of Christianity unless I questioned you about it. Christ, the Church, morality, confession and how did psycho-analysis stand in relation to them? It was a perpetual anxiety to me. When I asked you about some particular point, and the answer you gave seemed to be the opposite to the teaching of the Church, I would say: 'Yes, but what would Christ have said?'

I had been so fervent a believer when I was a child and adolescent, seeing angels through the plain lattice windows of the village church of my aunt, and at home, going willingly to matins and evensong with my grandmother, where I had visions of Christ passing down the nave. Altars covered with their embroidered cloths concealed the most precious treasure of the universe. I was always the only communicant at the early service on New Year's Day, and I accepted transubstantiation without question. The presence of Christ constantly by my side was what kept me alive. I punished and mortified my spirit so harshly that I was not strong enough to keep up with my intensely secret life of worship. When I was eighteen I broke, and I decided that what I had prized so highly was only emotional, and that intellectually I could accept nothing. One evening I became hysterical with weeping. My father came to see me and said I could only cry if I had a reason. I closed up entirely then. I had lost my faith. Even the visions which appeared before me shortly before his death – I dismissed.

Now I no longer think that way. I believe my feelings and emotions to be nearer the usually invisible truth than my feeble intellect and reasoning. I am not so ardent or faithful as I was before, and I am more full of sin, but Christ once again is everywhere. Rarely supporting and comforting me but His presence is a reality which I know I have to go far to reach. Whether you live or die, the journey is long, as Dante knew so well.

'What would Christ say?' It worried and troubled you how to answer me. You were so modest that you did not consider yourself knowledgeable enough or even worthy to discuss it. You did not believe in the Church as it stood. I think you saw Christ as merely an historical figure. You were dubious but always open-minded about life after death. You believed we made God within ourselves and within our imagination. Imagination is reality. Sometimes I felt that the whole subject when you thought about it, which was seldom because you were so strenuously occupied with living, troubled you more deeply than you would admit. 'I do not feel qualified to discuss it with you,' you would say. Eventually you gave me Jung's *Modern Man in Search of a Soul* to read. You hoped that it would help. I found it difficult, but it did help. It distressed me, though, that our beliefs did not run parallel. I write down this quotation. It is by William Blake. They are fitting words for you.

The worship of God is: Honouring His gifts in other men, each according to his genius, and loving the greatest men best; those who envy or calumniate great men hate God, for there is no other God.

The Angel, hearing this, almost became blue; but mastering himself he grew yellow and at last white, pink and smiling.

*

I write to you at some length now of my older sister because you were in the process, just before you died, of doing all you could to bring us together again. We have grown apart. I do not know how much of a loss it is to her but to me it seems hopeless and irretrievable. All our lives we have been such a support and comfort to each other, and we both agreed that alone we could never have withstood some of the blows we received. Apart from brief partings we met and were together every day since I was born. We were always very different, and she often bore a lot from me, but it never seemed to matter in the end. We had a unity which the best of sisters have – and not only out of necessity. Even when I married it did not change, except then the wheel turned and it was I who gave support to her. Now, in spite of her invitations to stay, I have lost her. She has grown a shell which I cannot penetrate. She closed up and went away with her husband. I do not know why, but no longer can I be alone with her.

You loved your brother, except for the times when he arrived at your flat unexpectedly. You loved him, and I remember you speaking so sadly when you told me how his only son had been drowned, as though he had been your own. Your brother lives in the west country too. Occasionally you would go to visit him.

You said to me : 'Of course I like to be alone with my brother sometimes. He and I were together long before all this marriage business started.'

To return to my sister. Once, long before, she had had the chance of a 'proper wedding'. She was to have married an officer of the Life Guards, the son of a friend of our father's. Everything was arranged on a grand scale but she did not love him. Three weeks before the wedding she came to me, throwing a shoe at my head, saying that she would not go through with it. It took great courage on her part to cause such an upheaval.

I wore the white bridesmaid's dress I was to have worn at her wedding, as my own wedding dress. I had no choice. I had only twelve hours' notice for my wedding at St Peter's, Eaton Square.

My sister married an old friend of Martin's and mine. They were married at Caxton Hall registry office. I was their witness with two of her husband's friends, Derek Quincey and his wife.

I already knew what a flat, prosaic and unjoyful procedure a registry office marriage is. Have they arranged it so on purpose, as a punishment for the rebellious? The gloomy rooms, more like an abortionist's waiting-room, the registrar himself, an over-cheerful merchant, badly disguised as a pastor, and the hurried words, spoken as though they will do 'until the next time'. People kiss each other and walk quickly out to allow the next couple to enter. Inferno, Purgatory, Paradise. I belong to the first two. Will one day my sins be washed from me, and a Virgil lead me to the third?

My sister did not expect a traditional church wedding, with all her childhood dreams coming true. But I do not think that she was prepared for Caxton Hall, and somehow I could hardly bear it for her. In spite of her often ruthless determination, there is a vulnerability in her which might break at any moment. When I saw her standing beside her husband in the registry office, I also wanted to cherish her.

To us unmodern children, the picture of our wedding day had been imprinted in our minds since we were old enough to play together.

'Tinker, tailor, soldier, sailor, rich man, poor man, beggar man, thief.'

'This year, next year, some time, never.'

'Silk, satin, cotton, rags.'

On and on we would jump with our skipping-ropes, inventing our own concatenations, and counting out the cherry stones, down to the smallest detail of the day which we had been taught to believe was the beginning of our happiness. When we were older, our father had told us to make the most of our time at home before we were tied for always to the kitchen sink. He liked to prepare us for the worst, not really taking seriously any alternative to marriage. He liked best to keep us at home.

After my sister's wedding there was a lunch in a restaurant. I sat next to Derek Quincey who I instantly disliked and distrusted. He was a psychiatrist. He made obscene jokes which I knew my sister hated. How unromantic he was, and to me he seemed conceited, considering himself to be avant-garde and so

liberal-minded. I searched in vain to find a hard core within him.
I asked him where he worked. He said at St Agnes's Hospital.
I felt myself freeze. I was filled with repulsion and turned away
from him. The thought of him being in any way connected with
you made me tremble. I did not speak another word to him, and
neither could I make myself say good-bye.

I gave my sister rose-bushes for her wedding present. They
were the old shrub roses: Rosa alba maxima and Celestial.

That evening I asked you whether you knew this Derek
Quincey. You said you had known him when you had lived in
North London. You admitted that you now considered him to
have gone slightly astray. That same evening it was your turn
to give the annual party for your colleagues in your flat. It was
an irritation to you but you always enjoyed meeting the ones
you liked and those whom you had not met for a long time.
You were social in the best of ways – a touch of the unsocial
being inherent in your character. I asked if Derek Quincey were
coming. You said that it would have been impossible not to have
invited him to this particular gathering. I felt the preparations
were pressing hard upon you. I would not allow Derek Quincey
to come. I would not allow him in your room, let alone sit in
my chair. You assured me that my chair would be put aside.
I became unreasonable and insisted on sitting at your front door
barring the way, and demonstrating against his presence. It
would not be long before the guests arrived but in spite of that
you remained patient. A small part of you agreed with me.
You persuaded me eventually to be liberal-minded in the right
way, and so I left.

It was nearly Christmas again. Perversely and childishly I
felt more than ever the absence of a family. Whether one wishes
it or not, one is swept into a wave of frantic festivity and
preparations for the uniting of families. I remember Gerard
saying after his children had been taken from him, that he could
not stand the sight of a Christmas tree. I know what he meant
so well. I had two houses which, entirely through my own
actions, stood empty. The vacant spaces – they worried you.
Once, Martin and I had had lovely Christmases in Scotland. I
was able to give children's parties then.

During the year I write of I developed a craving, a mania, to be included in a large loving family where I belonged. I became even more envious and angry towards the mothers holding their babies in the buses.

I liked making arrangements in your room. One day, without previously thinking of it, I went into the newsagent's shop, which was my shelter near to your flat, and picked out a selection of cards to suit my mood. All were brightly coloured, some with a high gloss finish, and others were raised and padded with shiny satin. They showed pictures of cottage hearths, holly, bows and hearts, and English-looking Alps. Each one was inscribed with suitable words of endearment: Mother, Father, Wife, Husband, Brother, Sister, Son, Daughter, Aunt, Uncle, and so on, until a large family had been built up. Some of them were scented with a sickly sweet smell, and were labelled 'perfumed' on the back. They were the more expensive. I bought a whole family and I did not allow you to look at them until I had gone. I had hidden them in your cupboard where you kept all your files, placing them in order of affection. My arrangement stayed, as my Leonardo postcards stayed on your bookcase. It made me feel better about Christmas. For the first time, I gave you a present. I hardly dared to give it to you in case you would not accept it, or would be embarrassed by it. I gave you the record of Schubert's Trio in B flat major. It was the old recording made by Cortot, Casals, and Thibaud. You were very pleased with it.

Martin gave me a painted fan behind glass. I gave him nothing, and it felt wrong.

When you went away you put your car on the train so as to avoid the icy roads. You said that you took particular care for my sake.

I spent Christmas with my sister and her husband in the country. My sister did everything beautifully, and I loved the children. But I could not communicate. You telephoned me several times, and I wished I was with you sitting behind the old cloth curtains of a certain rust colour, which you had taken with you to keep out the draughts. I went by taxi to collect Larissa for the day, meeting her and the foster-mother in the

84

nearest town. I took her back to my sister's house, and she was very good and sweet to me. She had a lot of presents round the Christmas tree. She was wearing her party clothes. She stayed beside me all the time. She did not want to play with my sister's children. They were much younger, and she was rough and aggressive towards them. She did not understand where she was or what I was doing there. She thought that I had taken the other children instead of her. She lay in my lap like a baby and said in a loud voice at tea, 'When can we leave this place?' I took her back in the taxi and returned her to the foster-mother. I have not seen her since.

When I went to church on Christmas Day, I discovered to my shame that I was jealous of the Virgin Mary. That is sacrilege. So I will write some words by St John of the Cross. 'Let a man first understand the invisible things of himself before he presumes to stretch out to the invisible things of God.'

I do not know how to describe the days and weeks and months of that winter, for mostly they were not times of exterior events which you can write as straight narrative. The scene was always there. Your room, with you sitting in your chair by your desk or at my side. So much of what we talked of can never be written. It was born and grew and developed but not visibly. There was no theatre. What was, remains within me, and will never leave for it has become part of me. There are great regions in what I write to you that must stay unexpressed. The poles of feeling, the best or worst, have to be left unsaid. There must be areas of silence. It has to be.

You told me that you went far beyond the limits of the orthodox, in time, action and speech. You led me into places of imagination which I did not know, and dared not believe existed. You began to liberate my mind. You and I were the participators. No one else. You started to remove great boulders of stone which I hid behind, refusing to move, until you so nearly rolled them away. You used a stern strength which is not force.

I was your infant and child. You were my mother, and father, and husband, and lover. You were my wife, and the times when I was a boy, a man, or a hermaphrodite, you were my brotherly

85

friend. You were more than all these too. More than doctor, teacher, and stalwart supporter. You were something more which must remain silent. The silence you would wish.

One day I told you that when your wife had died and you were alone and very old, I would come to your house in the west country, and I would put my arms around you and hold you very close, to comfort and protect you. I would not leave you. You often told me that I would be the one to leave in the end. There would have been no end, though, and never really will be. There will be no true leaving. When you were alive I believe you suspected that too.

The silence continued, woven into our meeting. Not known to anyone. Should they ever wish to know what the silence contained, let them listen to a fugue in the night.

*

Surely I should now be able to carry on and make the best of my life, even though you are not visibly here beside me. I try, and try, and I cannot. I make progress with my writing to you, but slowly and with immense difficulty. I shelter within the walls of the Klinik. You knew how much I hated it; not the people, but the atmosphere of suffering and mental illness. I am afraid of its infection, its almost insidious quality, which might hold me for ever. But it has kept me alive.

I try with the will-power of a general but I have been shot, and have an open wound in my stomach. When I go into the outside world to make contact with the brave and the fit, I limp along, fooling them for brief moments, and disguising the wound which will not heal. I have won races as a short sprinter but never as a long-distance runner. I fail. I fall. It bleeds and bleeds. I grow confused.

I have tried to put an end to it myself but they saved me.

The things I wrote to you yesterday filled me with joy but at the same time have given me a depression. The tears are running down my face and will not stop. I will continue with our last winter together tomorrow.

Today I am dragging myself over the *chotts* of the Sahara, with the salt and sun burning and scorching the fatal bullet hole. You always told me if it came it would be fatal. It came in the middle of the battle. Give me your very gentle irony. It is necessary to live and die with the smallest flicker of it somewhere.

It is Larissa's sixth birthday today. She is having a party in Somerset with all her friends.

I write fragments which occurred between us in our small, but at the same time ever expanding world. Fragments of that icy winter when spring never came to Bishops Road.

The smell of stews and cabbage cooking hung around the many passages in your block of flats. I was always catching colds. I asked you what you did if someone on the hospital staff came to you with a cold, and you said that you told them to leave the room immediately. You could not spare the time to be ill. I was afraid of giving you my colds but you were prepared to take the risk. Very occasionally you would get an infection and take a day off work. I asked you nearly every day whether you felt well. I knew that I tired you and I was terrified of your falling ill. You fussed over my health too, especially my eyes, telephoning Mr Lawson, the eye surgeon, if you thought there might be something wrong. You sent me straight to the hospital with a huge cyst on my eye, and directly to the doctor with a temperature of 104°. It was tempting not to take taxis while I was standing in slush and snow, with freezing winds blowing through the huddling people. But I thought of my accountant who was still causing trouble, and refrained. It was hard but a relief returning to the dark and empty house; a relief not to have to pretend. I wrote to Larissa's foster-mother every month, and she replied with news. I bought Larissa's clothes but no longer wrote to her. It apparently did not seem to mean very much to her. You spoke to her foster-mother at regular intervals on the telephone, giving advice and discussing any problems.

We talked endlessly of my house in Scotland. Should I keep it in spite of opposition? Never do anything hastily, were always your words. Sometimes you thought that I should get away from my family background, and that my house and the country around it were too full of ghostly images. But you knew how I loved it and you thought of schemes which might be fitting for it, however unpractical they may have been. You thought I was a good administrator. Perhaps I am, but it does not interest me.

I went on at you relentlessly. A question I have asked myself since I was seventeen. What is it that I must do? I must do something. My sister never understood what I meant by 'do'. I longed for a vocation; it did not come, and it was not there. It was a grievance to you how badly I had been educated. You repeated it again and again. I had been kept at home with governesses until I was aged fifteen because of supposedly epileptic fits. Mr Godfrey Morgan of the Hospital for Nervous Diseases had told my father not to send me to school, and to put me to bed every night at six o'clock. You were the only person I told that my blackouts and fits were self-induced, so that I could be touched, caressed and loved. I always deceived them from the age of five to fifteen. You understood but made angry sounds at the mention of Mr Godfrey Morgan's name. 'He would not have said the same for a child of a working family,' you said. I told you that my father had done his very best for me but you remained furious at the lack of real education and training I had received.

Sometimes at week-ends I went to read history to a man who had gone totally blind with glaucoma. It had happened to him a few years before. Now he was studying to go to Oxford, late, aged thirty-three. He passed his exams for New College and went there with his Alsatian dog. I admired his courage, and was pleased to help him in even the smallest way. To be truthful I did it reluctantly, boiling with frustration as I set out. To help a blind man who did not wish to be pitied, and whose plight might well have been my own. It was not much to ask. But sometimes it is not enough to help. It can make me angry and leaves me unfulfilled. One cannot force oneself to become a social worker. You agreed.

I worked and worked at 'Eleanor'. I wrote sixty thousand words, was utterly dissatisfied, and began all over again. It was the only thing which gave me any satisfaction.

There were many times when you criticized me. Spoilt in the wrong way, arrogant, haughty and obstinate, you said. I denied nothing. I learned about humility through you. It is a goal to be reached under many difficulties. Will I ever achieve it in its proper sense?

You had come to the highest nobility, and humility, through your work and natural gifts, not necessarily by birth. I could take any reprimand from you because it was always the truth.

You did your best to prepare me for the birth of my younger sister's baby. I was happy and glad for her that she was having a child but each day I saw her, the old pain and hurt returned. The pain of grief for my dead and unrecognized child. How small I am; but I do not see myself changing in that way.

You said every woman should have a child if possible but that it was not the most important thing in a life. Nearly every woman could have a child, it was no tremendous achievement. You told me that I was an individual who must cut out a mould and fill it with other things if I could not have what I wished for. You said what I put into that mould could be even more valuable. You thought if I did have a child as soon as it showed signs of independence and was weaned, it would be the same thing all over again as with Larissa. I did not agree. What you said made no difference and nothing will ever make it any better. I listened to my sister talk of cots and prams and feeding. I acted superbly. She had a son in the hospital where our father had died. I sent her flowers and some delicately-made night-dresses for the baby. It gives me pain and also pleasure to buy those baby clothes, and to send flowers to maternity wards. I smile, I rejoice. I grieve.

I have four, or perhaps five or six more years left to me, to be able to have a child. I do not have much hope although I am not barren now. That is the irony. Through the years of my marriage; secretly counting days, not daring to breathe or move, until the hysterical crying came of endless disappointments. Between, the operations. And at last I was cured, when it was too late.

'Stop pretending,' you said. 'For once, show your best friends when you are depressed.'

I cannot. I act. It is automatic. I am afraid of being thought 'gutless and lacking in courage'. It has been ground into me ever since I can remember.

Eleanor committed suicide in the end.

'Why,' you asked, 'did she not get in touch with a friend?'

You were a great believer in friendship in its true sense. But Eleanor could not have done so. There was no one there, so she ended it all, which was what she has unconsciously wished for the whole of her life.

When I was seventeen I wrote that I would commit suicide if I could have no children. To me, to be barren was the end of a woman's life.

One, two, three, four, five, six more years? Larissa's mother was forty-two when Larissa was born. I hate just the idea of her. That dark woman.

Ignite my life again to numb the pain. I will hold on to you and music which are my greatest loves; but repeatedly, stubbornly, I write what I wish –

> Watch – watch the waves break –
> Listen – to the sounding of the shingle
> On the shore. Shelter your child from the sea.
> Should it come to take him I'll grieve for you –
> So – mourn for mine too.

*

The cold days of Lent passed by. Easter was early that year. The usual question was turned over and over again. Where was I to go for those two weeks which seemed to me so endless and threatening? We drew blanks at every possibility. You agreed that the summer in Italy had been too much for me.

One day you said: 'How would you like to go to Switzerland?' You took me completely by surprise, and then I remembered the piece of paper with your address on it which you had given me so long ago. I still have it. It lies before me as I write. 'Hotel Waldhaus Dolder, Zürich. August 28th–September 5th.' I remembered telephoning you in Zürich from Scotland. I had only once been in Switzerland, when I drove from Basle to St Gotthard through the Ticino to Rome, with Martin and Gerard, in the Land Rover.

I looked at you suspiciously. You said that you had a friend called Dr Frey, who had a clinic in Zürich. I could stay in an hotel, the same one where you had stayed, which was of the undemanding type and comfortably old-fashioned. It only stood a hundred yards away from the Klinik where perhaps you could arrange for me to spend my days. My first reaction was, no. I would be too afraid to go alone and meet so many strange people. But I still asked you what it was like. You said that it was a large old house with a garden full of shrubs and flowers. The rooms in the house were big with high ceilings, and there was a workshop downstairs. I said that I could not imagine myself hammering brass but you said they had other things to do. You said that the patients there were like me, some worse, some better, but all having had nervous breakdowns and problems which had overwhelmed them. Most of them would get better but some might not.

'Who did you see there?' I asked.

'I saw a lady sewing,' you said.

That did not sound promising to me. 'What would I do there?'

'You could take the cable-car down the hill, and then a tram into the town with someone who was going there. Some of the patients are starting to go out to work. There are many good concerts and operas in Zürich, and you can go for excursions on boats on the lake. It is inclined to rain a lot there though.'

'Who would I sit next to at meals?'

'I expect to begin with you would be put beside an English-speaking person.'

'What about drink?' I asked you, making as many difficulties and obstacles as I could.

'Well, you could always buy a bottle in the town, and there is a large beech wood at the back of the hotel. The Swiss are so tidy that I am sure there would be those bins where you could put the empty bottles.'

'What if I felt afraid in the hotel?'

'There might be room in the Klinik but I believe that three or four people share a room.'

The few single rooms, you thought, were kept for the very

bad cases. Most of the large rooms were not adaptable to be made into single rooms, and a lot of people liked to share.

'I could not share a room with strange women. It would be far too intimate.'

You laughed.

Then you grew more serious. You said that the idea had come to you for a number of reasons. Firstly, you knew that I would be safe there. Also, you thought that it would be good for me to be amongst people again, but with people who would not expect much of me in the way of conversation. In other words I could be how I felt, without acting.

'And if I liked it, could I perhaps return so that holidays would no longer hold such terror for me?'

That was exactly what you had in mind. You telephoned Dr Frey in Zürich after I had left, and later in the evening you let me know that he had said that I could come. He would make arrangements for me to sleep in the hotel and to spend the days in the Klinik. He would be there only four days during my stay because of his two weeks' compulsory military service. There was a very good English psychiatrist though, quite new to the Klinik, who I could see instead of himself.

I was dubious about it all, but grateful to you for taking so much trouble. I knew too, without being told, that your thought also ran on other lines. An escape route – just in case? You had saved me but at the same time you had got me into a tight corner.

'Please don't die, will you?' I asked you over and over again. The burden must have been heavy on you. I knew that it worried you. 'What would I do if you did die?' I almost demanded an answer.

You gave me the name of a doctor who knew more than anyone what your work was about.

'Where does he live?' I asked.

'In Chester Square.'

His name remained in my mind. I was perpetually filled with fear. Where and to whom would I turn to if you died?

'It would be a disaster to your life,' you said. 'If I died, someone would have to look after you, that is all. But I am not going to die, that is why I take such good care of myself.'

People have different ideas of how to take care of themselves.

How would I get to Switzerland? I had often forced myself to fly, but had become increasingly afraid of it. 'One can never afford to be a coward in life.' My aunt's words rang in my ears. I found with relief that all the flights were booked, and I made elaborate plans to travel by train from Ostend.

'What clothes shall I take? What will I do when I arrive at the hotel?'

You were diffident about bothering Dr Frey, but you telephoned him once again. I was told to take clothes that I would wear in a small country hotel and, you added, with a frock to change into. I was to telephone the Klinik as soon as I arrived.

'What is he like, Dr Frey?'

You would not tell me very much. You said that his real name was Dr Frey-Wehrlin, and that the Klinik was the C. G. Jung Klinik, following Dr Jung's work and ideas as closely as possible.

You had been to Jung's funeral. You said that it was ghastly, with long panegyrics, which you were certain he would have hated.

'Did you ever meet him?'

'Yes, just once, as a mere underling.'

What were you? I never asked. Jungian, Freudian, Adlerian? You fitted into no strict category. You seemed to have made your own.

Zürich, the Klinik, and Dr Frey. I fussed and fumed, and questioned and objected for days and days on end. I did not think that I wanted to go. What if I never got back to you? Fear, hideous fear, grew in my mind increasingly. Not curiosity. You were the curious one.

Before I left for Zürich, I had a dream that the Klinik was run by women of the Gestapo, and of the s.s. Of course it was not like that at all. In fact it was the opposite. I have though, never forgotten that dream, and sometimes I have experienced fleeting moments which hardly exist, when the dream was not a lie.

I am so tired. I sleep and sleep.

I shall not write very much of my two weeks stay at the

Klinik in Zürich. I scribbled a diary each day I was there, impressions of the things I saw and heard and felt. They were many. I was only a guest though, not a patient, and I did not begin to understand what it was all about. It was like entering a strange and alien world. It was totally different from what I had imagined. You would never have known that the house was a clinic, although the front door was always locked, and only the privileged had keys. The rooms looked more like a nursery school than an institute for the mentally and neurotically ill. That impression was wrong.

I came to know many people, but not as lasting friends because at the Klinik there can be no such thing as true friendship. In its place there exists a tenuous bond of loyalty between patients; unspoken. I felt shaken. I did not understand. Above all, I felt the presence of the empty restless days, the silence at meals which was welcome to me, and the half-concealed suffering that I sensed in almost every person and corner of the house. I only stayed one night at the Hotel Waldaus Dolder where I had a lovely room overlooking the lake and the city. The hotel was as you described it. I liked it with its old-fashioned stuffy atmosphere, and its dining-room where no one stared curiously at one, because of their own melancholia. I was afraid and lonely though, and when I was offered a single room in the Klinik, I accepted it gladly. I felt cut off in the hotel and I wanted to be with people. Everyone in the Klinik was kind and friendly towards me. I heard nobody speak maliciously of anyone. It snowed every day; wet English snow. Time slowed down in the wrong way and the inertia was infectious. It became an effort to do anything. I went to the Kunsthaus. You had told me not to look at the Swiss pictures but at the French paintings and the Giacometti sculpture. I spent a long time there and bought you an illustrated catalogue. You were very pleased with it. You read my diary with interest. You knew all about my stay in Zürich. So much has happened to me here since that the thought of living through and describing in detail those two weeks again sickens me. I hated it. I cried every day. You telephoned me from England three times; but you were so far away.

I met Dr Frey the first evening I arrived. That, I will tell you

94

about. I was so thankful to reach you again that I never described precisely my first encounter with him. There are rare occasions when you meet someone who you know immediately. You recognize them. You can see into their minds. At once, yes or no . . . *Augenblicklich* is the most descriptive word I can think of. In these people passivity is absent. Challenge is present. In their eyes there is integrity, humour, perception and humanity. Whatever you say or write to them they will understand. Such men are very few, and I have yet to meet a woman of the kind. The *Blltz* in these men's minds is something to take notice of. Watch them secretly, hurl your spirit against them to steal the gold dust. Snatch at their wisdom. I say it again, seize the *Blitz* while you can. I cannot let opportunities such as these slip through my fingers, in this poor average world to which I belong. Dr Frey had nothing of the grim conservative look of the town-bred Swiss. I knew that he would know about animals and plants and the wind and the sky, and of their treachery. I asked him to excuse my bad manners but I felt impelled to tell him how much I disliked the Klinik and the atmosphere of Zürich and that I hoped I would never return. I thanked him for his hospitality and then I began to cry. I wanted and needed you so much.

'I wish he was here.'

Dr Frey took hold of my arm and my hair and twisted them until it hurt. 'Part of him is here.' He spoke with the toughness of a Highlander.

On leaving, he shook my hand and said, 'Tomorrow you will see Dr Carlton. He speaks perfect English.' There was the politest mockery in his voice. Directed to whom?

I left a day early. I could stand it no longer, even though it meant returning to an empty house before you came back to London. Without Dr Frey, the point of my being there went.

'Why,' I asked you angrily, 'did you not tell me that you had trained Dr Frey in London?'

'It was very kind of him to mention it,' was all you said.

I swore that I would never go to Zürich again although I had not left easily. It was the patients: the homesick or the hopeless.

I was not, I am not, and never will be a patient. I am a proper ordinary person. I told you a hundred times.

My return to you from Zürich was like a dangerous mission completed. Never had I been so relieved and happy to be with you in your room again. Everything was the same as I had always seen it. The familiar comforting things. The room which nothing and nobody, however passionately I may love, can detach and take away from me. There can be no healing, or transferring or mending with time. It is not because of any obstinate refusal on my part, for I am open. I am so hungry that I am dying for want of sustenance. I would give anything to forget you most of the time, and let you fade as a memory, and live. I live with fervour while I write to you but when it is over, the life and the fervour vanish into my ears.

I will try. Do not allow me to die, or to drop the burden. Help me to remember 'the yawning abyss within which despair carries on its game'* and that I must wait for the day when I will be sent death by God, to free me from the earth and from the body, as you have been; and that then there will be joy.

No, it is not any obstinate refusal on my part. It is you, and your sequestered room, where every object seemed to be threaded by a vein in your body, given life by your touch and blood, which none can wrench from me. To see you in the flesh, and to feel you near me, filled me with a love which can never be surpassed. Never suppressed or quenched or dimmed. It can only remain shining for you, such as you never knew.

That was how it was the day I came back to you from Zürich. You received me home with the same gladness. It was more parallel, and silent, than it had ever been. You said so.

The next day you had changed. You had become a completely different person. One whom I had never known; an aloof stranger. You were cold and formal towards me. I could not understand. I was shocked and broken. What was it that I had

---

*Kierkegaard, *Fear and Trembling*.

done? I knew that it had nothing to do with your other world and life. You would not have allowed that to come through, and even if it had, I would have known at once.

Often I asked you, 'Why are you sad? What is it that is troubling you?'

Frequently it was a difficult problem with staff at the hospital. Once a young doctor who had been about to start a new job and life with his family in Canada had just had a coronary thrombosis, and now his hopes had gone. That distressed you terribly. Another night you sounded so sad on the telephone that I asked you what was wrong. You said that a colleague of yours, an Indian woman with whom you had worked for long, had been having supper with you. She was leaving for India the next day to start a new life, and you knew that you would never see her again. Your voice was weary, and I wept for you that night. You never wished to tell me of these things, but I drew them from you. I would not let them pass. They affected me almost as much as they did you.

But what were you doing now? Why were you adopting this approach to me? It was not that you were being tough. I knew that basically, you were a tough and resilient character but not distant and frozen as now. You had turned away from me. You would not tell me why. I demanded an explanation but you persisted with this manner which did not suit you. It was a deliberate act directed straight at me. I cried and cried and rolled on the floor. You took no notice. Why were you rejecting me, and so soon after our coming together again? I was so afraid. I tried to cling to you but you would not let me touch you. I did not look at you when I left. I sat on the stairs outside your flat, numbed and unbelieving. It was the same on the telephone at night. This cool courtesy from afar. I panicked, and rang you again and again until finally you took the receiver off the hook. It was as though the disaster of all disasters had happened to me. Waking the next morning I felt an overwhelming fear and sense of loss before I realized what had happened. All that day I tried to work out in my mind what it was that you were doing. I came to the conclusion that it was an act and a trick, which perhaps was well-intentioned but not worthy of you. I saw straight through it, and that you would not be able to sustain it or carry it out. It was what you just might have tried in your much younger days, but you would have quickly discarded it as too obvious.

I went to you though, still afraid. What if it were really true, and you did not want me any more? Rejection by you, ending in estrangement for ever? Your sudden disappearance from the world, our world, which was the only one I had. I had a taste of what I had always dreaded. I lay screaming with terror in my chair, pleading with you to stop it. You did. You gave me valium, and a glass of glucose and soda-water which you took from your cupboard. I told you that I knew what you were doing, that it was beneath you and second-rate. I saw it all. You were trying to make me angry but all you did was to petrify me out of my mind. Gradually you became yourself again. You did not confess outright to me that day, but later you told me what I had guessed was true. You had hoped that after this last separation, which had been so different from any other, you might by your behaviour bring out the anger you insisted was in me, and there-fore start to break my total dependence on you. You said you had seen immediately that I could not endure what you had attempted. That anger and hatred. You had tried for so long, and it had never worked. It exasperated you. I knew that I worried you, but if necessary you were prepared to take time. All the time there was. Never again did you play tricks on me. You knew that I knew you too well.

Now I see that you also had fear at times, which you never showed. You did not wish to inflict such pain on me. But what if you did die? Were you in the last years of your profession allowing an analytic relationship to reach a point of emotion, that no one, not even you, could break? I shall speak no more of it. I have neither the right nor the knowledge.

As I left you that night, it was as though my heart had started to beat again.

*

April, May, June, July. Our journey continued. Secretly it progressed, but as I have said before, silent and undeciphered to the world. Fragments, sketches, impressions, are all that must be told. You painted your pictures in the greatest detail, but in writing of those months I cannot imitate your style. You would not wish it. As I write now, I shall feel each time the touch of your skin, or your coat, or the texture of an object in your room. I had gradually picked a large hole in the loosely woven tweed material on the arm of my chair. You had meant for a long time to get it re-covered. You said it looked so old and shabby, but I would not allow it to be touched. Instead it was darned with thick grey wool. I felt the stitches threaded in and out, downwards and sideways, competently patched. 'Your wife has mended it?' I was pleased. There were times when I wanted to go to her instead of you. I imagined her to be large and soft and protective. I wished to escape from the precipices, mountains, and the valleys were David met Goliath, and the deserts through which you led me. The pale green gardens and the fields of May, and the branches of apple blossom in the vase on your piano, were not always there.

Often on buses I would see a middle-aged woman and a young girl together. They would be going out shopping or returning home. Over and over again I would study their features, recognizing them as your wife and daughter. They looked so contented and intent on their purpose, as though they shared a bond. Once or twice I had followed them, and then had lost them in the crowds. If I happened to be travelling to see you, and two of them would be sitting in front of me on the bus, I would get off at the traffic lights and watch to see if they got off at the stop. Just supposing they did, and walked down the road, greeting the porters at the door? I would have been right. It would have been your wife and daughter returning home. I watched until I saw the bus go on, the two still sitting in their seats, going who knows where. How I dreaded confronting your wife and daughter, meeting them as hostile strangers at the door, their eyes seeing straight through me, shattering me to pieces as though I were made of glass. I never met them. I never encountered anyone. I only heard the footsteps outside your door. I either ignored them or remained silent. By acknowledging my silence you drove me to reality, which I had grown to acknowledge because I trusted you now. I had my place in my chair from which you had promised not to remove me.

One day I arrived and went slowly through my routine of taking off my skirt and folding it neatly on the piano-stool. I felt more uneasy than usual. You put me into my chair and immediately I leapt up. It did not feel the same. My cushion had been touched. I knew that there had been someone sitting there before me. There had been a strange presence in the room. Even the air had a heavy and peculiar smell. There was no cigarette smoke but it was as though there was fog in the room. I refused to sit down and I put on my skirt again and started to leave. You laughed. You could not help it. I knew that I must have looked a ludicrous figure. I was like an affronted cat who has lost her dignity. I began to cry. There had been someone there before me. You said that there had been. A woman you interviewed for the hospital. You had shown her to the other nasty little chair which had never been big enough for me, but she insisted on sitting in mine. For various reasons you had refused her the job. You said that you were sorry, and you opened the window to let out the foreign smell. I lay on the floor that day wrapped in my summer batiste covering.

You told me that at one time you had smoked forty cigarettes a day. I do not know why you told me at that moment. It was like a confession. You sounded guilty.

'I stopped because in the end I frightened myself,' you said.

I could not imagine you chain-smoking. The idea revolted me. Your whole personality would have taken on a different aspect. In return, I let you know that I smoked six cigarettes a day. I had never mentioned it before, and I had hidden my cigarettes in the bottom of my bag, or under the tins of soup and potatoes in my basket or old paper bag. You said that it made no difference to what you felt towards me. There were many other things which we exchanged. What a relief and delight it was to have disclosed the fears and tensions which I believed would have turned you against me.

Fat London pigeons sat on your window-sill. You hated them. They drove you mad. Every time they came, you said that you must put wire netting against the window to prevent them, but you never did. They made such a noise scuffling against the glass, like rats. You always knocked loudly against the window to drive them away. They paid no attention whatsoever, and made you look silly. I did not mind them. I watched them, fascinated. They pecked at each other right amongst the little feathers on their heads and round their eyes, either from love or searching for parasites. We stared at them, incredulous. You resentful. They made me feel like a voyeur. Then we laughed and laughed.

I have never enjoyed laughing with anyone in my life so much as with you. You laughed with the whole of you, quietly. I laughed with the whole of me, loudly. Clutch your stomach and let it ache!

I cannot write to you today. The ground is not sure enough beneath my feet. I know that it is not true, but the whole world seems to be shifting and sliding, and all I see is darkness. I feel that I am sinking. I have no confidence left. I saw Dr Frey this morning and I became so unsure of his taking care of me. I slept until four o'clock in the afternoon. Half in my sleep I went to the telephone in the *Apotheke*, and rang up Thomas at his office. He is living apart from his wife and family now. I hope that he is all right. I was afraid to write to him because I was certain that my letter would not be welcome. What gave me the courage to speak to him? It has made me feel no better.

Dr Frey will let me die. He cannot help or prevent it. He cannot keep me prisoner here for always, and it is my choice in the end.

'Help me.'

'Can I?' he said this morning.

That is what has struck me so vividly today. I am just another case in the Klinik; not as with you. Dr Frey does his utmost for me. I cannot stress enough how much he does for me, and I do not want to leave him. I learn from him and I am very grateful. But I am so afraid. You would be grateful to him too. I understand that maybe he cannot help me, and I know the reason why. The fault is mine. I fight and fight but my heart does not seem to stand it like the more faithful. If I had a strong branch to hold, then I could succeed for you. I do so much want to. I must not give up and fail.

Please God, release me from this life where I love too much.

I must start writing to you again after relapsing so badly yesterday. I have to do so to be with you, or else I die from our parting.

Last night I went to the window and wished to throw myself out. I reasoned that it would do no good. I would end as a helpless cripple while the unfortunate people caring for me would pity me, hiding their impatience. There would still be nobody there. I felt so afraid that I asked to be strapped into bed. Then I looked at your photograph, studying each feature one by one, and mourning you. I am here, and you are gone, but you have not left me. I must wait. That is what life is; waiting. While I wait impatiently, I must work. I must not allow my fervour to abate, for that is depression. I must live fervently, as you showed me how. Every day I must say, 'Do not care if there seems to be no one there. Defy. Defy the depression of emptiness and longing and fear, for I belong to you, and you are with me.'

It was in May that Nan's sister Jessie died. She was eighty-two. I felt happy for her, and also relieved that she would no longer be my responsibility, a continual pricking of my conscience. Then after a day or two, I fell into a deep depression. I did not know what it was about. You told me it was Jessie's death which had caused it, although that had not appeared to touch me very much. I write this story now, because in the end it brought out in you a 'letting-go'. A moment when we shared grief which was not only mine. A completely different grief but alike. Death, after all, is in common.

Nan, who I loved almost next to you, died when I was fifteen. I loved her green eyes and her large comfortable body. I loved to kiss her face which was covered in prickly hairs. She was very brave. She survived a disastrous train crash, and, although shocked and wounded, she carried straight on with her journey. She died slowly and painfully of cancer at the age of sixty-one; all the time she still joked and made friends and struggled to knit clothes for me. She devoted her life to me since the moment I was born. I was the object of her adoration which I returned to her in my own way. She came from a true cockney family, living north of Hampstead. Her father was a cabinet-maker, who was so strict and possessive that he prevented his five good-looking daughters from ever marrying. I cannot write much about Nan because there would be no end. She spread affection wherever she went with her clowning and stories and humanity. She spoiled me, and told untruths to protect me. She was easily hurt and was very emotional. Three times I saw my father make her cry. Those were some of the unhappiest moments of my childhood – as though life had come to a halt. One night when I was home from school, the telephone rang. We were all at dinner and my father answered it. He returned and continued as usual but I half-knew what had happened without being told. The next morning he summoned me to his working-room.

'I have bad news for you, dear, Nanny died last night.' He spoke with difficulty. 'I do not expect you will want to go hunting today. Just go for a ride if you wish.'

I stood silently in front of him for a moment, and then left the room. I hid myself upstairs, and was rent in two. My father drove me back to school that evening. Nan was never mentioned. My father and my older sister went to her funeral, but I was not allowed, in case it made me ill. When I told you about it you were furious. You could not understand how I could have been sent back to school that night.

'Of course you should have gone to her funeral. You would have been put through it for a week or two but you would have come out better in the end,' you said.

Hettie, Cissie, Jessie, Lily and Elizabeth. Elizabeth had died in her early youth. Lilian Blanche Long was Nan. She died at Cissie's home, Malt Cottage, in the west country. Cissie and I wrote to each other frequently after Nan died, and I visited her twice, sleeping in Nan's bedroom, drinking cider at supper, looking at the rows of runner-beans growing in the garden, and listening to Bach's Air on the G String on the old-fashioned H.M.V. gramophone. On both my visits, we went for an outing up to Dunkery Beacon in an ancient taxi. She had once been a music teacher; then she had become a companion to a Miss Young, who was very old, and who left her Malt Cottage when she died. Cissie was more severe and had none of the cockney strain of Nan. Every year I sent flowers on Nan's birthday, 19 September, for Cissie to place on Nan's grave.

Hettie was a moaner, so Nan said. She was an upholsterer in Hampstead by trade.

Jessie was a domestic in London. During the war it was she who came to meet Nan, my sister and me at the London railway stations as we travelled from aunt to aunt, or grandmother to grandmother. It was a certainty that Nan would lose the luggage, and my sister would cry, and Jessie would give us a packet of sweets. As the train drew out of the station, Jessie would run down the platform waving good-bye, and then return to the bombing. Nan rummaged in her bag and brought out an apple and a small knife. 'Like a bit of apple, ducky?' and then she started to talk to whoever happened to be in the compartment. Whispering, she told them that we were motherless. It was not interesting but she always made them interested. It was a gift of hers. My sister went red in the face and pretended to disown her, and I put on my dressing-up hat which I took everywhere with me. 'Crazy Kate,' I shouted, trying to obliterate the whole situation. But Nan would go on until we reached our destination.

After those terrible journeys, I lost touch of Jessie until I started to go and see Miss Lane at the Clinic in North London. Cissie had written to say that Jessie was not well and was unable to keep her own flat, and that she had been moved to an Old People's Home. I went to visit her on my way to the Clinic in North London. I recognized her immediately, although it was more than twenty-five years since I had seen her. The same rather sad-faced lady, now over eighty, in her long print dress and straw summer hat, sat waiting for me at the gate of the Old People's Home. I believe that she always had a melancholy, amounting to discontent and self-pity, which neither Nan nor Cissie possessed. But now she was crippled with arthritis and very unhappy. She was without hope.

I looked at the Home and I could see that she was pining away. I could not allow her to stay there. I could not let her perish amongst the grey surroundings. I could not leave her to suffer under the coarse harshness of the matron of whom she was afraid. I found her a room in a house run by a society for elderly people. It was in Hampstead which she refused to leave, having lived there all her life. There was a resident housekeeper to clean and cook, but to a certain extent, the residents had to be capable of looking after themselves. The doctor confirmed Jessie fit for this. The room was unfurnished, and as all her own furniture had been taken from her I bought her new things, and a bone china tea set to which she had been used. The room was large and sunny, overlooking a garden, and I made it as pretty for her as possible. But I was worried at taking the responsibility of moving such an old lady. I hired a car and took her for a drive round Regent's Park and Queen Mary's rose garden. It was a Sunday, and in the evening we went to the church which she had always attended when she was able to travel alone. She missed it more than anything. It was a Baptist church in the City, and the Welsh minister stirred the large congregation as few Anglicans could do. Jessie looked happy. Afterwards she took me to the social gathering in the modern building underneath the church. Everybody was welcome. A large group of German students, married couples, tramps, and anyone lost or in need of company.

The deaconess of the church, Sister Joan Hadley, was Jessie's friend. She was quite young and I was filled with awe at her gaiety and dedication. I saw her alone in her office. She said that she had never seen anyone with Miss Long before. She was surprised and curious. I explained to her briefly what I was intending for Jessie. I asked her if she would consider sharing the responsibility with me. There was so much to do, apart from furnishing her room. Dealing with the Old People's Home, acting as sponsor, pensions, insurance, wills, and many other things, all of which I had not really the authority to undertake for Jessie's safety. Sister Joan agreed to do so.

I helped Jessie to move. She still had her own bed and eiderdown, and huge wardrobe of clothes some of which I remembered as being Nan's. I hoped that she would make friends with the others in the house. Sister Joan was to share the visiting with me, and she arranged for her occasionally to attend the church. At first Jessie was happy; too happy. It was not a success for long. She made friends with an old man next door to her but he died, and she said that the others in the house were below her class and manners. For weeks, I was unable to visit her myself because I was in hospital. During the winter, her arthritis grew worse and she fell. She was sent to St John and St Elizabeth's Hospital which, to her distaste, was Roman Catholic and run by nuns. She returned to her room but became more and more lonely. She had not the capacity for friendship like Nan. My visits to her became more and more difficult. The bus rides there were long and cold, and she was full of complaints and worries when I arrived. She sat in her long dresses and pinafores in a weary depression. She was extremely trying, and she exasperated and saddened me.

Finally she could only walk with the help of an aluminium frame, and she could no longer dress herself. The Society wrote and asked me to remove her to a Council Home. The matter was put into the hands of a Welfare Officer. A modern Home in Lewisham was found. Jessie did not want to move from Hampstead. She said that Lewisham was on the other side of the river where she had never lived. Sister Joan and the Welfare Officer and myself eventually persuaded her, having first taken her to look at the Home. Only clothes, photographs and a few ornaments were allowed. Jessie was distressed that she could not take her bed. I packed her belongings. I bought cardboard boxes and suitcases to fill with what was left of the trappings of her life. Her best dress had to be placed on the top and not on the bottom, and there were piles of old-fashioned underwear and hats which had never been worn. She hid her money in her travelling-clock, in case they took it from her. She was angry and afraid and possessive.

> Où serez-vous demain, Èves octogénaires,
> Sur qui pèse la griffe effroyable de Dieu? *

I saw them during my stay in the geriatric ward in St

---

*Baudelaire, Les Fleurs du Mal.

Stephen's Hospital, this last March. 'If only the Almighty would take her,' a younger one whispered.

Jessie was contented in the Home in Lewisham. She liked the people, and she enjoyed the food. Her character seemed to change. She did not complain any more, and she would be smiling when I arrived to see her. She even talked of visiting Cissie in the country.

I did not look forward to the visits to Lewisham. I went by bus which took nearly all the day. You told me that during the war you had worked in Lewisham in an old Victorian hospital. As I travelled I used to watch for the hospital where you had worked. I imagined you bicycling from Lewisham to the centre of London, which was what you used to do in your free time. The small hospital was a building typical of the Industrial Revolution, and I could see you setting-out from there, bicycling through the grim suburbs, not paying much attention to air-raid warnings or the bombing. You would mostly be wondering what you were going to make of your work. And you would have been planting the seed of your genius for understanding children. I expect you would have stayed too late in London, and then made a fuss in case you did not get back before the black-out. I am sure your bicycle would have been an old one, heavy, and with constantly puncturing tyres. Those dreams of you bicycling to Lewisham helped me in my bus rides to Heath Rise, S.E.13.

I loved to make Jessie happy, and to telephone Cissie afterwards to tell her that all was well. But to my shame I still bore that resentment and frustration in myself.

Then Jessie fell and fell again, and went into a depression. The Home said that they were not alarmed, so I did not make a special visit to see her in the middle of the week. She died one night in her sleep. Sister Joan, as her executor, made the funeral arrangements, and I telephoned a woman in the west country asking her to break the news gently to Cissie, who was lying ill and in pain. I was to meet Sister Joan at an undertaker in Lewisham, and then we were to drive to the crematorium. Sister Joan was to take the service, and I was to be the congregation. You said that you wished you could come with me. You knew what it would be. It would be Nan's funeral. Sister Joan read the twenty-third Psalm which had been Nan's favourite, and I felt as you had said, that time had turned back, and I was at last attending her funeral. Cissie's flowers were left on top of the coffin, and also those from Hettie which had been sent by the Home she was living in. Hettie was ninety-eight and was blind and deaf. Afterwards we went to the Lewisham Home to go through Jessie's things. We left everything behind except for some photographs of Nan and all her sisters, taken when they had been beautiful girls, and also some photographs of my sister and me when we were children. There were two little china vases missing which I knew had been Jessie's favourite possessions. I asked for them. The matron produced them guiltily. Perhaps she was keeping them for herself or to be sold at the Home's jumble-sale. I gave them to Sister Joan.

We returned together, by train to Charing Cross. Sister Joan looked tired. I wished to offer her a holiday in Scotland, and for her to take a friend to stay in my house. It would give her the peace and the rest that I felt she so badly needed. I did so afterwards by letter, but she replied that she had been chosen to represent her church, as the only woman officiating at the services at Oberammergau. It was to be a working holiday. I told you that I wished I could be like Sister Joan, and I still have not learned that I have not been made that way. As I left her at the station I said: 'It seems a strange question to ask because I know you so little, but do you believe we see those we love, again, when we die?' She hesitated before she answered: 'I would not like to say, but I believe so.'

Last week I heard that Cissie had died. She was ninety-two. She had the courage and determination of all her family, and each of them went through much sadness. How many packets of letters have I from her, ending with such words: 'May God bless you, dear, and bring us happier days. If we put our trust in the Lord, He will take care of us.'

In the evening, after Jessie's funeral, I went straight to you. I took you the photographs which I had collected from the Home in Lewisham. One of them showed my sister and me sitting on a piebald Shetland pony. The pony was called Dolly. My sister was five and I was two. My sister wears a tweed coat and leggings, and I, a white coat and bonnet trimmed with fur. We seem to be in a park in the country in Northamptonshire. My sister is smiling to the camera and I am looking cross. Nan stands by our side wearing her felt hat and her grey costume. Her feet in their lace-up shoes are pointing outwards. She always said that she walked at a quarter-to-three.

When I was ten, Nan was sent away. They thought that she was spoiling me. She was to return for short stays during the holidays. I never said a word, and Nan tried to conceal her feelings for my sake, although she had cried and cried when Dad dismissed her on a holiday picnic in Cornwall. It was a terrible terrible thing. Nan was gone, and an elderly governess with dyed hair, came in her place. We were to call her Corkie but I never called her anything but Miss Corke. She filled me with hatred and repulsion. I remained silent to the grown-ups. But alone with my sister, on a walk to the village post-office, I clung to her, and screamed in sorrow in the thawing snow. My sister did her best to comfort me, and we bought a tin of potato soup with our pocket-money in the village shop. We ate it with our fingers, in the bushes in the garden. I ate it nearly all, filling and stuffing myself with the cold gluey mixture. I could not eat enough, so badly I needed Nan. I wrote of my grief in my diary, in a code of my own, so that no one should read it.

After the war, while our father was recovering from malaria, we went with him to live in Scotland. The governess came with us. I had lessons with my sister in the schoolroom. The governess chain-smoked with yellow fingers and drank black coffee and coughed. She put me to bed at six o'clock every evening and in the afternoons made me lie in the dark for two hours on the floor. It was the doctor's orders which Nan would have disobeyed. For some reason Miss Corke became obsessed with me. A pathetic and revolting possessiveness. She said about my sister: 'One cannot touch her with a barge pole.'

I hated Miss Corke with all my strength. I became naughtier and naughtier, hiding from lessons, taunting her, and spitting into her face the stewed apples which she tried to force down me. One morning she was found dead in the schoolroom. She died from a cerebral haemorrhage. While her coffin was taken away, our father sent us for a walk on the hill. We stood in the heather looking down at the house. It lay far below us. We watched the coffin being carried out of the door. It was put into a hearse which then drove away. We were afraid. But suddenly we were overcome with joy. I slept that night in the room next to my father. He was to take care of me; and he had sent for Nan. She travelled overnight and arrived the next day. I met her in the dark kitchen passage, and I threw myself into her arms. We clung to one another, and she never went away again, until she became so ill.

You listened about Nan attentively, and also about Jessie's funeral. You began to tell me quite a different story but one with a similar motif. I have not many details to write, and I did not know who you were describing until many weeks later. It was the effect it produced in you which marked me, and which comforts me now profoundly.

You had told me before that your own mother was very good when you were a small child, but that as you grew up she had not been so understanding. As a young man, you took a room in a large house in Cresswell Place that belonged to a woman who let rooms to students. It was not a boarding-house, it was a family home full of people who knew one another. You had stayed there for a long time while you were studying and taking examinations. You enjoyed the life with the other people, and the woman became like a second mother to you. She had two sons of her own and was married to a violinist. Her husband was constantly unfaithful to her. Finally, she left him.

'And if you please,' you said, 'she took him back and looked after him when he was old and ill, and nursed him until he died.'

It struck me then, that in spite of your kindness and forgiveness together with the training of your profession, there was a strict morality bred into you. If I were able, would I not do the same for Martin? There our difference lay. It was more than just a moral code. You could not live with anyone, whatever the circumstance, if you, yourself, did not feel them to have a basically truthful character. It distressed you too much. You could not tolerate it, in the past, present or future. You sat at your desk, looking out of the window. You told me the story of the woman who had been such a mother to you, and who you had loved so much. You had never lost touch with her. You sat for a long time looking out of your window. At last you said: 'She only died last year, and she had been swimming in the summer off the coast of Boulogne, at the age of eighty-two.' You turned towards me and I saw that tears were running down your face. 'Now you have set me off,' you said, without trying to stop them. 'She had a memorial service in a small church in South Kensington. I read the lesson, something which I do not normally do. I do not know why she had a memorial service. She was a Communist.'

We had shared grief, and I shall not forget it. On the way back in the bus I wondered as I so often did with fear, of your dying, and what your funeral would be like. The thought was in my mind over and over again, uselessly.

I have just come across some words which perhaps even you would not have minded to have spoken. They are by Hermann Hesse, translated from the German. They are for you.

—a spirit of serenely cheerful and brave piety, a superbly chivalric morality. For in the final analysis every important cultural gesture comes down to a morality, a model for human behaviour concentrated into a gesture. As we know, between 1500 and 1800 a wide variety of music was made; styles and means of expression were extremely variegated; but the spirit, or rather the morality, was everywhere the same. The human attitude of which classical music is the expression is always the same; it is always based on the same kind of insight into life and strives for the same kind of victory over blind chance. Classical music as gesture signifies knowledge of the tragedy of the human condition, affirmation of human destiny, courage, cheerful serenity. The grace of a minuet by Handel or Couperin, the sensuality sublimated into delicate gesture to be found in many Italian composers or in Mozart, the tranquil, composed readiness for death in Bach – always there may be heard in these works a defiance, a death-defying intrepidity, a gallantry and a note of superhuman laughter, of immortal gay serenity. Let that same note also sound in our whole lives, acts, and sufferings.*

---

* *The Glass Bead Game.* Translated by Richard and Clara Winston. p. 44.

Last night I did not sleep at all. I sat in the *Apotheke* with Schwester Bernadette, watching the dawn rise, and listening to the hundreds of birds singing. I knew it was beautiful but I could not find it so. Dr Frey told me it was Midsummer eve, almost as though that had something to do with it. Perhaps it did; there is a magic quality about that night. Good or evil.

I feel depressed. I have just woken at seven o'clock in the evening. Topsyturvy. I feel half in a dream too, so I will only tell you a short story about Nan, which I forgot to tell you before. Then I will leave her, although I do not want to. The story epitomizes the greater part of her character. It is a topsyturvy story.

My sister and I and Nan were making a visit in the country. There was an evening when we were invited to see a film, shown at the big house. The King and Queen were present. The King was wearing a tartan dinner-jacket.

'Well I never,' said Nan, loudly enough for everyone to hear. 'Just look at that! His Majesty is wearing my travelling-rug.'

I end now. You always said of a day which appeared to be upside down : 'Pack it in.' However much they cajole and entice me into the world, all I want is to be enclosed in sleep, hoping to reach to wherever you are.

The King expects everyone to do his duty. I know it.

I have just found you, in Schubert's Octet in F major. I stand at attention before you, looking straight into your eyes. I listen sternly to the music, which is made from dances.

*

Every day I worked on 'Eleanor'. How could it be that such a short story would never come to an end? Would I ever finish it? I tore up pages and rewrote them, over and over again. It will never be perfect, exactly how I want it, or truly complete. It still has no proper title. I must leave it how it is now, and continue to write to you. That is like a compulsion inside me. What if nothing comes? Then I die a death of unproduction. Each day I fear it will happen, and the tension which holds me will subside for ever. For me, that is the most precious thing I possess. It keeps me alive for you. The people I associate with affect me. That is why I shun society in its worldly sense. I try to become like the people I meet in it; and then I break because I fail. I must have the right driving force behind me, and perhaps one or two people. I must live in the right house, wherever that may be?

I bought a copy of the score of the Eroica Symphony. There is a scene in 'Eleanor' where the music is briefly mentioned. I was not sure what it would sound like played by instruments other than those for which it was written. I took the score to you, as I have no piano in my house. I asked you to play me the Trio from the Funeral March, to see how it would sound without a full orchestra. I had so often wished to hear you play. The piles of music lay on the top of your piano, tantalizing me every day. Occasionally I heard a note or two through the front door of your flat. You would be playing or practising for a few minutes while you waited for me, but it was not loud enough for me to hear. You took the score from me. You put on your glasses. You said that you did not think you could possibly pick out the tune. I knew that you could sight-read perfectly well. Your hands shook. Could it have been that you were nervous of failing in such a small thing in front of me? I could not believe it. Was it because music to you was such a personal and a valuable thing that you hated to expose any inadequacy on your part in public? To me? I could not understand. After a lot of hesitation and fussing you began to play the notes of the Trio. The triplets in a major key are unbearably tragic, coming directly after the slow, heavy rhetoric in the minor. You faltered but went on. The trotting of the plumed horses drawing the coffin. The music is too much. It came out on your piano just recognizable – those endless triplets which hypnotize. You became more confident and they began to flow.

Dr Frey has told me that he twice listened to you lecturing; once in London, and once in Zürich at the International Congress of the Association for Analytical Psychology. He says that he always thought of you as being a private person, but in the lecture hall you became something else as well. Your low voice carried in a way that everyone could hear; instead of speaking outwards to the audience, drilling what you had to say into their heads, you drew them into you, making them lose themselves in your realm.

Every evening when I returned from you, I would not inhabit my own house. I switched from the particular life we led together to your other world : I might have supper with you and your wife, a quiet family meal; sometimes you would invite one or two guests; I accompanied you occasionally to a play or a concert. During the evenings my own independent life did not exist. Even if it were after midnight and I had fallen asleep, you telephoned me and turned my hours of fantasy into reality because I persuaded you to describe what you had been doing in as fine a detail as you would.

Most evenings you sat until late at your desk. 'This is an age of paper,' you said resignedly. Other evenings, when you had not too much work, you watched television or listened to a concert on the wireless : the Diabelli Variations or a film about the life of John Clare. When I telephoned, I always asked : 'Are you listening to something?' If so, you told me what it was and I listened or watched too, and you would telephone me when it was over. You were a severe critic. You seldom went out to dinner, but very often to meetings. 'I think I will come with you,' I said, without any hope. When I returned to my house, I tried to imagine you with large groups of your colleagues, but on these occasions I got lost. In what manner would you move among them? What was your social manner? Did you have one? I would not have thought so.

The bus journeys were always the same. Sometimes there would be a quarrel involving a coloured immigrant or an episode with a drunk or a mad person. Every evening the bus went round Sloane Square. Round it would go, and the next evening round. In the light or the dark, the cold or the heat, in snow or rain. Sloane Square, even if I did not consciously think about it, always opened a scar. It was there that I had met Thomas the day after our very first meeting. That was twelve years ago on a hot summer day. In the bar of the Royal Court Hotel, we were persecuted by people we had seen at a party the night before, and we had to escape to the pub across the road. I had met Thomas so often in Sloane Square. Once I had said good-bye to him at the entrance to the tube station after a walk in St James's Park on an idyllic spring day. We had not met alone for four years. I tore a weeping willow twig off one of the trees in the Park. Thomas said that he would never forget me or what we had had from the beginning. We walked to the tube station at Sloane Square and I held the willow twig tightly between my finger and thumb. He brushed my hair from my forehead and then disappeared into the crowds to return to his work.

Since the time when it seemed I had ruined our relationship, I had tried to block Thomas from my mind. He would have to remain a painful memory. I did not talk of him even to you. But Sloane Square was always there. The tube station, the bus queue and the taxi rank. I found myself automatically searching faces in the crowds of the rush-hour.

'Why is it that I never see you amongst the people in the streets?' I asked him long ago.

'You never meet those you want, when you want,' he had said.

Sometimes I would see a face with a look of his. I would start, but I was hardly aware of my constant search, so little hope I had. So many people, so many buses and taxis, so many minutes to time slip.

One evening I was sitting on the seats which face each other in the bus. I was wedged into the corner. I was wearing a red scarf on my head, and tear-stains striped my face. The bus stopped at Sloane Square. People fought to get into the number 22 which came so seldom. Thomas was there, in front of me. I looked away and pretended not to see him. He was pushed to the front of the bus where everyone was standing packed tightly together. He looked back, and then looked again to make sure that it was me. I had less than a minute to decide whether to get off the bus before it reached the street where I live, shutting my eyes to him, or to make some gesture towards him. I could not prevent myself from looking once again. He pushed his way to me, and we jumped off the bus together. He seemed nearly as incredulous at seeing me as I was at seeing him. Our conversation was stilted and abrupt. He told me that he was not very well. His marriage was at breaking-point, and he could not see any way but separation. I could not think of anything to say. We went and sat in a pub. He had not much time. He said that he had not been in touch with me because he was obsessed with his family problems. He left me at my house, embracing me with his extraordinary affection, and saying we would meet again; I felt that an enormous burden had been lifted off me.

As I write, I am half-listening to Bellini's 'La Somnambula' on the wireless. I was introduced to Thomas by Martin, for the first time, when I was twenty-two, at a performance of the opera at Covent Garden.

You were wary for me, always.

*

There was a production of *Uncle Vanya* at the Royal Court Theatre in Sloane Square. Uncle Vanya was to be played by Paul Schofield. It was an occasion not to be missed. I bought a bunch of tickets the first day the box-office opened, knowing that the run of the play would be sold out very quickly. I did not quite know what to do with them. I asked friends, but they were either going to be away, or they had other engagements for that evening. I did not really want to go with anyone. I wanted to go alone; perhaps that was why I had also bought a single ticket for a Saturday matinée performance. After a great deal of thought and summoning of courage, I asked you if you would like two tickets to go with your wife. I knew that you loved Chekhov; and this was going to be something very special. You showed pleasure at my offer, and regretted having to refuse, but you were going to the country that week-end. It was true, of course; but was there not a crossing of lines which you were so against, feared almost, as an ingredient in your refusal?

You were going to stay with Dr Adler for the week-end. You telephoned me from his house. You told me before that you enjoyed going in the summer when you could sit in the garden, but the house was so small that in the winter it gave you claustrophobia.

As the characters from Chekhov long despairingly and passionately to escape from their crumbling provincial lives to the society of Moscow, and to have their unrequited loves fulfilled, so I, too, had always wanted to go with you when you went to stay with Dr Adler. Away from the city, which disintegrates people instead of making them whole, breaking them into fragments like a china cup thrown against a wall. I would be like the Chekhov characters in reverse; and for a few moments reach my goal. Dr Adler, you and I, would have tea outside in the garden, just the three of us, surrounded by bushes of the old shrub roses. I would listen as you talked together through the summer afternoon. There would be a table with a cloth laid over it, and a tea-set, and thin cucumber sandwiches made of brown bread. I would store what was said in my mind for the future, the winter months, when the heads of the roses would have faded and dropped, and have been drawn under the earth as the dead. You and Dr Adler in his garden. That was my Moscow. Why was I so obsessed with the talk and the tea outside? This is the reason why. Apart from the pleasure of sitting with you in a hidden wild garden, so unlike Bishops Road, I would have learned perhaps more in a few hours than I would ever have learned in my life. I would have laughed, too, amongst the roses, because there would have been happiness.

I have heard it said somewhere that criticism is a delicate matter. I have read somewhere, too, these words: 'The conventional romantic English upper middle class interpretation of Chekhov's characters which turns despair into nostalgic melancholy, and quirky hopeless action into lovable eccentricity.'

I went by myself to see *Uncle Vanya* on the Saturday afternoon. It was in a small setting, not as the Russians produce, but very beautiful. At one moment in the play, Uncle Vanya shoots at his hated brother-in-law from the city with a pistol. 'Bang! Missed? Missed again! Damnation!' he cries in drunken despair. I laughed too much, and people turned to look at me.

In the final scene when Sonya, the niece, is left alone with Uncle Vanya, all hope lost of their desires coming true, she says that if they wait and work patiently for long enough, one day they will see the stars as diamonds in the sky. 'We shall rest! We shall hear the angels, we shall see all the heavens covered with stars like diamonds, we shall see all earthly evil, all our sufferings swept away by the grace which will fill the whole world, and our life will become peaceful, gentle, and sweet as a caress. I believe it, I believe it . . . Poor, poor Uncle Vanya, you're crying . . . You've had no joy in your life, but wait, Uncle Vanya, wait . . . We shall rest . . . We shall rest!'

You told me that a violent thunderstorm broke while you were sitting in the garden with Dr Adler, and the roof of the house was struck by lightning. You returned to London that evening, and so did he.

*

We often talked about the Klinik in Zürich. You knew how much I disliked the Klinik and the suburban streets. You knew that I hated the city with its sterile lake. But I always told you that I liked Dr Frey, and sometimes I said: 'I wonder what he is doing, now this minute?'

I had felt there was something Chekhovian about life at the Klinik: a group of people, all longing to escape from a life they found intolerable, but none of them sure that if they took the step forward, their dream might not turn into illusion. Time ticking slowly by. People sighing, swearing, crying at its slowness which seems merciless, without end. The games of dice and poker, and when they tire of those, the talking and talking, without coming to any possibility of a conclusion. It was like the repetitive circle of an alcoholic, and a way to pass the time. It drove me to distraction. I would never return. I think it disappointed you a little, how strongly I felt about it. Was not the Klinik a stem from you? You would not have thought of it in that way. You had hoped that I would have regarded it as being a place of refuge, if necessary. You stuck firmly to your opinion that however I may have hated it, there was something which still drew me there. I could not disagree. The Klinik has a pull; it does not let one go. But it made me suffer a pain and loneliness quite different from what I knew with you. The infectious lethargy. That frightened me the most. Days, weeks, months, years could be spent in the Klinik without producing anything. Never would I return.

Occasionally I asked: 'Do you think Dr Frey liked me?'

'He did not tell me anything to the contrary,' you said.

I had had two small things to do when I returned to London from the Klinik. Sven Hansson, a good young Swede from the country, decided to become a Montessori teacher, and to do his training in London. He produced a blank card and a typewritten envelope giving his name and address, and he asked me to send him details of the Montessori centre in London. I was to write immediately, the day I arrived. I did so. I also sent him a short letter, saying that if he came to London I hoped he would visit me, and I thanked him for his kindness in the Klinik. He had tried his hardest to please me, and to show me Zürich. I never received a reply. I did not really expect one, but it distressed me.

The other request was from a man called Lechleitner, who came from Illinois. He had been in the Klinik for five years, and regarded himself as 'head'. He would not be moved from his opinions. He could not be moved from his ways. The Klinik had become his home. He organized reading circles. He baked bread every Wednesday, dressed as a chef. He went shopping for the Klinik, buying honey and olive oil. Every evening he read the Psalms in Latin and English, and he sat in his rocking-chair singing the religious songs which had been taught to him by his mother long ago. He criticized other people. He had taken me to church, and out to lunch in a restaurant, and to the station when I left. He told me his story and I had seen despair for one moment in his eyes. He had a dream of creating a semi-religious community with the help of his father. He wanted it to be in London which he had never visited. Please, he asked, would I send him a large map of London, marking the quietest and most agreeable areas in which to build. He gave me a Swiss cheque to pay for the map. I told him that he could buy one in Zürich, but he insisted it should come from London. I asked you which areas you considered suitable to mark. You laughed, but not unkindly. 'Piccadilly Circus,' you said. I sent the map, and shortly after received a reply written in huge handwriting. Pages were covered and the writing was in an old-fashioned Quaker style. It was signed Dr Lechleitner. He had passed his medical exams in his youth, and was entitled to call himself, Doctor. I showed you his letter. 'He thinks he owns the world,' you said.

I had told some of the patients at the Klinik that I might possibly return for my holidays in August. It made saying goodbye easier, and it was as though I were not abandoning them for a life which they might imagine to be one of happiness.

I told you I did not understand how it could be that some of the analysts at the Klinik could have meals at the same table, not only with one of their patients, but with several of them. In public view, talking and laughing, and passing the salad. It had astonished me. I felt shocked.

'It is a different thing there altogether,' I said. 'A totally different thing.'

You agreed, without any trace of amusement in your voice. You regarded the point as a serious one.

If our relationship had been exposed to a crowd, it would have been damaged; not broken, because it was strong and unbreakable; but it was of such a rarefied quality that even in the atmosphere of a closed clinic it would have been stricken. Only under our own terms could it grow. It might have perished under a public glare because it was so real and true. There was no pretence. I would like to write these words in capital letters: stop searching for a phenomenon like you because to do so will be my destruction.

I told you that Dr Frey does not attend meals at the Klinik. He is not public. I would despise him if he were.

Once again I cannot continue with my writing. I feel too sick today. I feel sick in my heart and my whole inside, for what they did to Magda, the American girl. We are in the same room. She has been very depressed for two days. This morning Dr Carlton was beside her bed, showing solicitude towards her. Choosing the right cards for her as she played patience, and discussing the tapes of classical music he had lent her. So nice and kind, but with the forced kindness that someone might show towards a trying child they had been landed with for the day. There were no threats or admonishments or suggestions that she might need help. Suddenly at lunch time, without any warning, she was strapped into the belt and given an injection. I am not qualified to argue what was best for her, but I fail to understand the way in which it was done. Her screams, her tears, her struggle. I know them all, and I became her in her agony. Gaspar Sanchez came to comfort her. He is a junkie, and if allowed, would poison himself slowly to death at the age of twenty-two. He is gentle and understanding and has great depth, and goodness.

You could show a firmness and strength which I could never bend. But can I imagine you ordering such a thing as I have witnessed just now? Where, where, is your tenderness? Are there none left in the world who are true, and most important of all, abiding? Is there no trust left, in the darkness, without you? Today is a beautiful day in June. The trees are calm, and overflowing with sap, but I scarcely notice them. I can see now why I cannot stop grieving for you. Oh, for your tenderness which soothes my soul instead of bruising it. It was you who knew what to do with the strife of the human heart.

Last night I danced. I enjoy dancing more than any other pleasure. I danced with no one in particular, just for myself, at a party in the town where they spoke Spanish, Hungarian and German. I was delighted that I was unable to join the conversation. I danced away from the straps, and belts, and depressions, almost into an ecstasy of freedom.

That is how it was with you one day. I had been worrying about the holidays, that never-ending problem, which grew in size every time they came round. We had fantasies of me taking Larissa and the whole of the foster-family to Scotland. We dismissed the idea very quickly. Larissa had just had her fifth birthday. I sent her a wig-wam, but the station did not deliver it in time. She had a proper birthday with a party.

It was a hot afternoon and the pigeons were scratching on your window-sill and puffing themselves out. Both of us were tired, and tensions were stretched too tightly. Trouble seemed to be mounting, exactly what I did not know, but sometimes I felt that there were things beyond our control. I became so distressed and angry with myself that I beat my head against your cupboard and tore out my hair. You hated me to harm myself. I was always doing it, and it seemed to hurt you more than it did me. I did it at week-ends when you were not there, so that you could not prevent me. That afternoon I ripped my dress, and then my stockings, tearing them again and again. They hung on me in rags, destroyed for good.

'You stupid little fool,' you said. 'Look at you now. How do you think you are going to get back like that?'

After a storm between us you went and fetched some safety-pins, and you spent over half-an-hour pinning each tattered piece of cotton together. You worked with great patience. I took off what was left of my stockings and put them in my bag.

'You will have to take a taxi tonight,' you said.

I must have looked like some 'Crazy Kate' patchworked together, with the safety-pins glittering all over me.

It was not really the mounting strains and stresses which made me behave in that uninteresting manner. It was that I suddenly tired of, was infuriated by all the unnecessary clutter of civilized life: clothes, shoes, bags, oddments of cosmetics, shopping baskets, tins of food; all the things which people are supposed to be unable to do without, but which at that moment I loathed. They trap, and encase, and get in one's way with their encumbrance. Most of all, I hated my blue and white spotted dress; so pale and pretty and correct. I sensed that you did not like it either.

There were many afternoons when I was sickened by what appeared to be my useless possessions. Bits and pieces. I wanted to be rid of them. 'Consider the lilies . . . ' the phrase had been passing through my mind for months. While I was working at something it had kept coming up, appearing from nowhere, and it had never occurred to me to remember its meaning. 'Consider.' No translator could choose a better word than that.

∗

I had known for long that you would be gradually taking on less and less work and would be retiring from the hospital in the winter. You had already stopped your afternoons at St Agnes's in the West End.

'I got fed up with that some time ago,' you said. 'But I still enjoy using their printed writing-paper.'

I minded a great deal that you did not go there any longer. The Lyons tea-shop below. It was at St Agnes's that I had first met you, and I so long to relive that day. I felt glad for you but at the same time resentful that you were retiring from both hospitals. But you needed to rest. The pressure of your work had made you look far older than you were. You had given so much of yourself to the hospital; and what did they give you in return? On the coldest days of winter, when your car had broken down, you had to travel to work by bus, which involved many changes, waiting around and walking through snow and ice. Could not the hospital have sent a car for you? You expected no special service. You just cursed your old car.

For the moment, I have to stop writing. There are two scenes of hysterical crying going on which are being treated with what seems to me unjust severity. This is a room close to hell today. I am not strong enough to stand the sickness and sorrow of this place. I am not like you. I cannot bear the things which you also could not bear, but you could contain them within yourself – usually. Except for the story you told me about the father and daughter who had fallen in love, and how the father had ended in prison. You found that hard to contain.

It will be difficult to leave Dr Frey and I am afraid to do so. But I am unable to stay. I shall finish writing to you in some other place if there is no time here. I shall live with all you gave me. I shall try as hard as I can because I love you so. It is the grief of the world which kills me. I have not the strength to carry it for other people, let alone myself. Laugh with me some time but not just now. I weep for them. I wonder, did you really know how much I loved you?

A very sick girl has just said: 'I have always believed in God until today.'

Last night, after I had written to you, I could not sleep. I sat in desperation at the round table on the landing. Thoughts of destruction went through my mind. Thoughts which I had not reasoned with. I was going to the highest window of the building to throw myself out. Anything would have done to obliterate the anguish of the days and the nights and the days, until death. Suddenly Dr Frey was there, coming up behind me, like he does, to surprise. It must have been nearly midnight. I have never seen him in the Klinik at that hour. He had come to see about someone else but it was as though he had come to save me. His presence calmed me after the horrific day. My sorrow subsided. It gave me peace and hope that he was there and had not deserted me. I believe that you had come, through him, to comfort me. I believe in such things with no sentimentality. This was reality. I had not dreamt it. Dr Frey told me so this morning.

You had a dream of the house you were going to build. A dream that was also a reality. That was where I broke off in my writing yesterday. You told me about it reluctantly. Someone had left you a piece of land which lay not far from Holland Park. You were planning to build a house which, owing to the size of the site, would be extremely small.

'When I stop working at the hospital I do not wish to go on paying for repairs for the leaking roof of this old place. I do not want to pay rent either. The ground is a gift and the house will be something of my own. It would be a mistake not to take the chance. It will be very small, all on one floor, but I need no more, with the house in the country.'

'Will you be able to take your cupboard?' I asked you, looking at the massive carved oak piece of furniture in whose patterns I traced my fingers. 'And what about the fireplace?'

You said that there would be no room for the cupboard and the house would have no fireplaces. It did not sound suitable for you. You assured me that your piano and your books, your desk and your paintings, would just fit in; also my chair and my footstool.

'It will not happen for a long time,' you said. 'These things take an age, what with plans and architects and builders. You need not think too much about it.'

'Will I come there just the same?'

'Of course, it will make no difference.'

'I don't want you to move.'

'I know. In many ways I'll be sorry to leave too, even though this place is falling to pieces. I am only telling you about it now to prepare you for the distant future. It will not happen for at least a year.'

I felt glad for you, but once again I resented it. I was ex-

124

tremely anxious. I hate to move and I think you did too. I kept very quiet. On the way back in the bus I tried to work out the route to your new house. I found the idea insupportable. I put it from my mind.

Again, I had failed to ask you the question I had always wished to ask. I had often reached the point of saying: 'There is something I want to know. Can I ask you?' Then I had never been able to continue. I could not and I did not – ever. I had heard before I met you that you had once been divorced and that you had suffered greatly. I did not wish to know about it out of curiosity. It was that I could not bear to think of the pain you had been through without my understanding. But it would have seemed impertinent for me to question you about such a thing. I think you knew all the time what it was I wished to know so badly.

One day you said: 'Dearest Sarah, if I do not tell you of things concerning my life it is not that I wish to exclude you from them, it is just that they would not help you or do you any good.'

In some ways I am a callous person but I could not tolerate the thought of your damaged heart. I did not think about it very often, but from our very first meeting, I had sensed that it had been battered and battered.

I could give you nothing in return for what you gave to me. You said that I did, by paying your fees which were necessary to you. I did not show it but it always hurt when you said that. I believe you intended it to, slightly. But I never needed a reminder of our professional contract. I was more than aware of it. Cringing away.

A divorce long ago; and the absence of your flat. Nothing can divorce me from you. Dr Frey came to me when I needed you so much last night.

'I cannot bear their unhappiness,' I told him.

'This is a house full of unhappy people,' he said.

That is what you would have said. You did not live in dreams.

'For someone like me,' you had said, 'it would be impossible to buy a house in the centre of London.'

I turned away from you. How I wished I could give you

everything I possessed. To give you everything and relieve you from anxiety. But I knew you would not want it. 'For someone like me.' Your words made me feel sick. 'For someone like me.' That was what made you what you were and is why I have only felt at home with you. Work, regardless of prosperity or ambition, unspoiled and unquestioning, and taking great pleasure in the smallest things. You said that you liked money when it was there, and its absence irritated you, but not unduly. You certainly did not live in dreams. You were simply untouched by worldly things. There was no pious martyr in you. You had a crossness which could be described as wrath. There lay your magic, which is lodged in the centre of my heart.

Tonight I am going to a lecture in the town given by Laurens van der Post. It has been a struggle for me to decide whether to stay and write to you – and the desire to do so grips me with a growing sense of urgency – or to let one evening pass and go to the lecture. It concerns stone age man. The subject does not fill me with enthusiasm. I suppose because I know so little about it. Dr Frey says that nothing coming from Laurens van der Post could ever be boring.

I have chosen to go to the lecture for a number of reasons. I knew that you greatly admired him and I see similar qualities in both of you. I met Laurens van der Post long before I met you, and he struck me as being perhaps the most remarkable man I had ever met. When I was twenty I had not met many people of his kind, and I have learned that one does not, even later. I sat next to him at a dinner-party in Scotland. I knew nothing about him at all. I just felt that I had found one of those who I was constantly searching for but never found. I do not know how the subject arose but he said to me :

'Have you ever watched the big cats in the Zoo? Watched them closely? Sparrows fly into the cages. They hop around pecking at bits and pieces. The lions lie lazily, ignoring them. The tigers just slowly blink their eyes and follow the birds' quick movements. They are bored by the sparrows; but to watch them is something to do. When the sparrows alight behind the bars where the leopards are sleeping, they wake at once and with one movement, pounce. Leopards will attack any living thing. They are the only cats with this in them, something which can never be tamed.'

'wenn dieser Ruck ein Blitzlicht in ihr Hirn wirft'*
'when that jerk shoots like lightning through their brains'.

That is what Laurens van der Post meant. It excites me so much. In one of his books he describes a scene in his prison camp under the Japanese. Its theme is defiance against fear and terror and pain. That is also why I am going to the lecture tonight. You would think it feeble of me not to go. I am feeble, that is why I have to go. You would have gone, of course; but out of interest.

I shall go again tomorrow to hear Laurens van der Post speak. The reason is not only because, after all, I found his first lecture interesting – more interesting than I have found anything since you died, when the sun went down for me and has not risen since.

. . . I need so much the presence of Dr Frey to keep me living. You knew that he was different, one of the people for whom I search. That is why you sent me to him. 'Sometimes I imagine you living abroad,' you once said. But I know I have to face the world without him, even now you have died because I do not belong to this country and have no place here. That is my predicament. The time is drawing closer and closer and although I long to leave Zürich, the thought makes me ill. Defy fear. It is easy to write it . . .

The other reason why I have to go again to hear Laurens van der Post is that, more than anyone I have ever seen, he resembles you. I could not remember what he looked like from so long ago, but as soon as he walked on to the platform in the lecture hall, it was as though I were seeing you again. The same frail build, the brown suit, the slightly cat-like movements. Oh, I cannot go into it all; he is not you. But to see him standing there gave me such a shock that I could not control the tears which persisted in running down my face for the whole two hours he spoke. I could not sleep last night for the vision of you he had

_____
*Rainer Maria Rilke, *Requiem*. Translated by J. B. Leishman.

conjured up in me, and because of the imagery of his language which could have been yours. The roots of his thought are of your kind; and perhaps one should allow Jung a say in the matter.

A reason I am going to the third lecture is because of a story that Laurens van der Post told last night. He was speaking of primitive man in the Kalahari Desert. Apparently they are very self-conscious about their short height and size, and, if you wish to make any contact with them at all, they have to be greeted with the words in their own language, 'I have seen you from afar, looming up over the hill,' in order to make them feel like giants. At first, a particular Bushman was hesitant. Then he struck his spear into the ground and went towards Laurens van der Post, greeting him with the words: 'I was dead. Now that I have met you, I am alive.' Those same words are all I can ever try to give you.

Last night at the end of his lecture, Laurens van der Post, having illustrated that in symbolic, primitive language the soul, to a man, is always feminine, and a daughter, quoted from Francis Thompson's 'The Kingdom of God' a line which astonished and comforted me so much.

> 'Yea, in the night, my Soul, my daughter,
> Cry, – '

I am the daughter of your soul, and your soul is in me. I know it without question, and I believe that you knew it too. It may sound bold of me, but it is not wishful thinking. I know it. In so many oblique ways you told me yourself, usually guarding your words to keep me from a dream world. It was no dream; I say again you knew.

> 'Yea, in the night, my Soul, my daughter,
> Cry, – '

The words followed me back to the Klinik. When at last I slept, I dreamt that I was in the middle of a waste land. I cry in the night as your daughter, searching for your soul in me.

*

It is tedious to state again that long before your summer holiday was due I was filled with anxiety. I had been invited to Italy again, but I knew that I could not manage all the people. You agreed. Neither could I manage my house in Scotland, with which you also agreed. I did not wish to bother you too much, but secretly I despaired of the time to come. I tried not to think of it. I had relatives, but you did not really wish me to be with them. I had thought of staying in London, perhaps getting a job as a manual worker in a hospital, or if not in London, in Bristol, which was within your province, but still a long way from you. You suggested other places which would be close to you. There was a bus, but jobs in those small country towns might be difficult to find. Our ideas were muddled and vague, almost without reality, and at times they unbalanced us both. For a while we did not speak of them although every night they went round and round in my head. Between us it was as though they had been forgotten.

Then one day you said to me: 'I would like to tell you well in advance that I have decided not to take a holiday this year. I shall stop work at the hospital for a week or so but that is all. I wish to go straight on with you without any break. It is the only way I can in the end, make partings for you, however short, more bearable.'

After my first reaction to your words, which seemed to sweep through me like a wind that took away all trouble, I looked at you. I could not believe what you had said. Your face looked tired.

'I will not allow it.' I told you as an order. 'It is absolutely necessary for you to have a holiday, and if you have decided this entirely for me . . .'

You said you were not only thinking of me. You had many worries, and things to do with the plans of your new house. I only half-believed you. I knew that there was something preying on your mind and wearing you down. But what could you do by staying in London, when all the people involved in planning and building your house would most probably be on their holidays? In my weakness I accepted what you had said, silently and then in tears. What joy, what truly heavenly joy, if I were to be at that moment of time now. I must curb myself from saying such things but try as I may, I cannot. I break.

'It will make you ill if you do not have a holiday,' I said.

'No, I am quite well. And I do not like August as a month anyway.'

What else is there to say now?

During the summer I am writing of, I was lying one evening on my bed, wide awake. It was still light. Suddenly the room became dark, and like a night sky without any stars or moon. In the darkness I saw some horizontal and perpendicular lines. It was not the sign of the cross, but it could have been a cross taken apart, and lain at angles away from one another. The colour of the lines was brown, and they had the depth and softness of velvet. As a good abstract painting becomes an object or being in its correspondence, so these lines were a young man I had known who had died the previous winter. He was them. I do not know how long this remained in front of me, but it told me that all was well with him; everything was perfectly all right. And much more than that. I knew him very little, so why him? I do not know.

While I search for your presence in everything, all I find at this moment are these words by Tennyson:

> Dark house by which once more I stand
> Here in the long unlovely street,
> Doors, where my heart was used to beat
> So quickly, waiting for a hand.
>
> A hand that can be clasp'd no more –
> Behold me, for I cannot sleep,
> And like a guilty thing I creep
> At earliest morning to the door.
>
> He is not here; but far away
> The noise of life begins again,
> And ghastly thro' the drizzling rain
> On the bald street breaks the blank day.*

---

* 'In Memoriam'.

I do not, and must not, and will not forget music. Mozart's String Quintet in G minor. K.516.

I had done all I could with 'Eleanor' and apart from some corrections it is completed as far as it will ever be. I began to write other things, not stories where one has to describe people and relationships which I cannot manage, but short poems, working at them over and over again. They were not real poems. But they obsessed me. I could think of nothing else, in buses, in the streets or anywhere I happened to be. Gratification combined with dissatisfaction. Each time I finished one, I was terrified that I could write no more. And why were they so small? I am afraid now, that after I have finished writing to you there will be nothing left. I will be hollow. I fear and fear that there is nothing there.

During the hot afternoon every barrier between us had been broken. I could sense your heart against mine, united as any hearts have ever been, both in pain and in joy. As I left you, you leant against the frame of your front door, supporting yourself wearily on your arm. I looked at you for longer than usual before I stepped through the door. I was saying to myself: 'I fear and fear that there is nothing there. I am not strong enough to do without what most people have, and if I have it, it gets broken. Please may there be something there.' I brushed my head against your arm which was my way of parting for the day.

'It is a tragedy that it is not me.'

You spoke as though you were thinking to yourself. I did not believe that you had said it, but you had; with a divine kind of bitterness.

I was in a state between reality and unreality, after I left you. When the bus reached Sloane Square, Thomas was there again, standing in front of me. I think that he found it strange but he would never have said so. Once again I was filled with disbelief, but now I had a serenity in me instead of the turmoil of the time before. He asked me to have dinner with him and said he would come to fetch me in an hour. In a not so foolish way, I felt I was betraying you. On the telephone you said you were glad, and that you would be there if I were to need you.

I had dinner with Thomas in a restaurant where we ate

outside. I felt shaken when I saw how unhappy he was. He has usually a reserve and an ironical turn of mind which are never broken in public. Work is a panacea, he says. He told me that he had not yet decided whether to join his family on their holiday abroad. He did not know what he was going to do. We talked about you, and of your daughter, and of his daughter, Patricia. As we walked back to my house, it began to rain. It was warm rain, and enjoyable, but he would take off his coat to put it round me.

'I think I am in love with Patricia,' he said.

'I've always known that you were.'

At my door I began to say good night. But he stayed with me. I was able to bear with that parting because although I loved him as I have always done, I was lost in you.

*

At two o'clock one morning, I was woken by a dull thudding sound which came from the window. I had been in such a deep sleep that I ignored it and slept again almost immediately. I had heard cars and a lot of noise in the street. People would be coming home from parties. A little later I woke again and sat up in the dark. I heard the door open, just a crack. Then I heard a rustle of paper. I always keep a paper-bag on the landing outside my bedroom door to put my rubbish in. Something must have touched the paper-bag. I felt that someone I could not see was watching me through the slightly open door. I could feel eyes looking at me. I began to sweat. Whoever it was, I knew that they were going to do something. I turned on the light by my bed and picked up the telephone.

Without actually dialling your number I said: 'Yes, I will expect you in a few minutes. Just let yourself in with your key and come straight up.'

I put the receiver down and waited, trembling. There was no sound. I walked out of the room and turned on the lights. I looked in cupboards and behind the curtains. There was no one there. It had been my imagination. I walked down the stairs. All the lights were on. I did not like that. I always turn off the lights at night. I returned to my bed and went to sleep.

In the morning I found that the iron bars protecting the windows in the basement had been bent and wrenched from the walls. The window had been smashed and dirty newspaper lay on the kitchen floor in order to soften the sound of falling glass. It took me all day to get bolts put on my bedroom door, windows nailed down, and measurements for new bars taken.

All this annoying business made me late for you. We tried to work out why it was the burglars went away and did not attack me. Someone arriving in a few minutes? You said that they could possibly have been soft-hearted, and could not have brought themselves to harm me. It was a nice thought but extremely unlikely, although you refused to dismiss it. It was typical of you to insist that I have a buzzer worked by batteries fixed under the carpet on the stairs. I hated the buzzer and I have never used it. It makes a noise like those in small news-agents' shops when the shopkeeper lives upstairs.

'This is the end,' you said. 'You are not going through another winter alone in that house.'

I made no comment, but I asked you whether you thought they would come again that night?

'No, not tonight,' you said.

•

They took Verena Sprüngli to Burghölzli today. Verena has been in the Klinik for over six years, but during the last months she has become so sick in her mind that they can do no more for her. She needs special treatment which can be given in Burghölzli. Nobody in the room knew that she was going. Neither Magda, nor Judy, nor Gaspar, nor Verena herself. None of us knew of it. Verena could not have taken the knowledge of it in advance. Dr Frey could not have told her until immediately before her departure. She has a horror of the place.

It was like a cortège; her going. Dr Frey, Frau Dr Holz, and Herr Stieler were her escorts. She had been strapped in the belt for six months and has suffered much every day. She is tortured in her mind. But the parting . . . However greatly she suffered, the Klinik had become her home. At one time, she had found happiness here with the things which were familiar to her, and with some people she loved. Her mother died last year, and her old father came to see her every day. She wants to be able to visit her mother's grave. It was she who said not long ago, 'I always believed in God until today.' Perhaps she will find God again, and herself.

The shock, the leaving, and the separation. It struck terror in me. Her cries of helplessness. I cannot stand up to parting from those I love and I felt Verena's suffering so. After she had gone I wept for her. All the separations I have known and those that Larissa has already had, surged in me. Dr Pestalozzi's great dog jumped on to my bed and licked my tears. Whenever I cried, my cat used to sit on my chest and wash my face with her rough tongue. Her kitten never did. He remained a baby and his mother always washed him until he started to clown again. Their cries were different; full of pain but without tears. Screams are of wild animals.

I am leaving the Klinik on Tuesday. I am going to London and Scotland. I have not been to Scotland for more than a year and a half. This time, I have been in the Klinik since March. It is now July. In some ways, I want to leave the Klinik but I do not want to leave Dr Frey. He and I have a contract that is only to be mutually broken. The contract says, that I return to Zürich after three weeks, to finish my writing to you. I am tired now. I need to rest. The most difficult part in writing to you is yet to come. I will not take an overdose of sleeping pills while I am away. However happy I may one day be, suicide will always be a battle with me. It is there all the time, and is a constant fight. Had you not died it would have receded, but now I must be continually aware, in touch, keep an image in my mind, and allow your soul to rest in peace. I do not trust myself. They are only words, although ones which I believe in. I am afraid. Do not leave me. Please stay by my side and lend me your courageous heart to beat in mine.

*

I have returned to the Klinik again after six weeks instead of three. During those three missing weeks I got lost, the thread was broken. I became unaware and also desperate, as though dying from starvation, and I fell. All the time I was away I kept thinking of your heart beating in mine; giving me the courage and the strength which I do not possess. I managed only for the three weeks of the contract between Dr Frey and myself. Dr Frey was right.

I left here in a thunderstorm, after a night of such terrible and sad happenings that the doctors' and sisters' nerves were frayed to a point of collapse, although they tried not to show it. My own anxiety at leaving was so strong, and the atmosphere of tension so infectious, that I smashed a glass-shelf in the bathroom and I nearly had a row with Dr Frey.

'Do not let us part like this,' he said.

'I cannot win.'

He said that generals may lose battles, but they have to win the war.

*

Somehow I managed to get out of bed and catch the aeroplane. All the lights went out at Zürich airport and the thunder seemed to be breaking right over my head. After five months in the Klinik, and the parting, and the screams and tears of the previous night, I did not dare to return to my empty house in London. I telephoned Thomas from London airport before he left his office. I had dinner with him. I could not remember how long it was since I had seen him. Now I know it was just after you died. I could not remember very much of that evening. I was in a different world from the Klinik but I still felt its terrible power pulling me in all directions. I was determined never to go back to Zürich, but I knew I had a contract with Dr Frey. I was sure that I could finish my writing to you anywhere, although the most difficult part lay ahead.

I was excited by new freedom. Thomas was depressed. But nothing went wrong between us. It was as if we had met the day before.

I went to my house in Scotland. My stepmother came too. I organized repairs and worked in the garden, and visited the people I had been afraid to meet. The garden was like a thing gone mad. The trees which Martin and I had planted had grown beyond recognition. There is a large bush of Portugal laurel around which I had planted pampas-grass and Rosa filipes, Kiftsgate. The plumes of the pampas-grass stood against the shiny leaves of the laurel, and the cream flowers of the rose hung all over the bush. Rosa filipes has flowered at last; after five years of waiting. It smelled of strawberries. I had no idea what it would look like; the laurel with the pampas and the Kiftsgate rose. It looks both strange and beautiful, but also crazy and unnatural. It gave me an uneasy feeling that I had started growing such an unbalanced and almost humorous thing.

One evening the sun shone on to the field in front of the house. The grass was a preternatural green. When that light comes in that particular country, it is a light quite its own. Then a huge moon appeared and I have never heard such silence. I did not even hear the sea.

I wished that I felt stronger. I got very tired. I was nervous and could not sleep. I did not believe that I could live there alone. But where would I find again what I was leaving behind?

Three times I tried to telephone Dr Frey at his house in the mountains, but the Scottish exchange could not get through the Alps. Once I heard his voice but he could not hear me.

When I returned to London, I thought that I had been living a false happiness and a false reality.

I made a new friend. I met Mark Chantler again. He had been brought up in Scotland where he had known my father when they were both young. He lives in the west country, but he was in London taking care of his mother who was very old and ill. He is a zoologist and a botanist and a musician. In his youth he had studied music in Paris where he met Dinu Lipatti. Together they used to search through Scarlatti's sonatas to see if they could find a boring one. They never did. That was one of the things he told me during those weeks. We met very often. He seemed to want to help me, and said that I should not be alone.

I enjoyed the day I spent with him and his wife and youngest daughter at the Zoo. The giraffes and the zebras together. Can you imagine the patterns and colours and proportions? The Zoo amazed me as though I had never been there before. The fish, the birds, the reptiles, the mammals. The small nocturnal creatures. Life everywhere, in so many different forms. The life force.

We were taken behind the snake house. Written in large red letters on the walls were notices for the keepers. 'If bitten, sound alarm bell, and lie down quietly in a safe place.' I do not know why I found that so funny. I had what Mark called 'Japanese laughter'.

I looked for my Peking robin and my fruit sucker which I gave to the Zoo some years ago. They were not there. Perhaps they had died, but Mark said that some little birds live until they are twenty years old. There were several birds which he had given, and they even appeared to know him. They pecked at his fingers through the bars, but they would not look at mine.

One evening we were dining at Claridges, and he was telling me about the humming-birds and the vampire bats he had brought back on his expeditions for the Zoo. The bats had to have blood lollipops in the aeroplane to keep them quiet. The air-conditioning in Claridges was not very good, and I looked at the steak on my plate and thought I was going to faint.

But all these days I knew and knew. I was glimpsing a unit, a minute section of a reformed sophisticated society, of a certain kind, in one particular country. I do not lack gratitude or affection, but without fully knowing it, my heart was sick for you. You, who had no special kind of background to fight up to, or down to, where sophistication did not enter your world, and reality was where you stood. All those things I had found and lost; and I forget that they are now always within me. The world rushes over me and sweeps me to the ground. I do not explain myself well.

I went to lunch with friends who live not far from you. I think that they, too, were anxious for me not to be alone. How difficult it is for me to go that way, where I see your flat in the distance.

Once again Maria and Richard invited me to stay in Italy, and I was pleased and accepted.

I had telephoned Dr Frey at regular intervals. He said that if I felt I could manage to stay away from Zürich, it was best for me. He talked about my writing to you, but he did not mention the contract he and I had made, and I respected him for his flexibility of mind. I felt wrong and doubted though, and I arranged to stay in Zürich for three nights in an hotel on my way back from Italy.

I made a visit to my aunt in the country. Martin returned from Spain.

You see, you see. Where was I? I had lost you, and my identity. I became so out of touch that I broke. I scattered into a million pieces. I had not written to you. I had taken my writing with me wherever I went, but I had not dared to look at it. Why was it?

I exploited Dr Frey's kindness, and telephoned him in the middle of the night, long after I had gone to bed. I told him that I would take the early flight to Zürich in the morning. Every minute I was becoming more and more engulfed and swept under by what I want so much, but fight against so hard. I telephoned Martin, who came immediately. I could not pay very much attention to him. I looked at your photograph; but something too strong had taken hold of me, and I took the thirty sodium amytal which I had been keeping. I knew that it was you who had given them to me. After a few minutes I remembered nothing. Martin got me to St Agnes's Hospital in his car. My heart stopped beating, but they put me in a respirator, and attached me to a cardiac machine in an intensive care unit. Afterwards, I thanked them, but I did not mean it. That is all. All over again. Forgive me again for failing. For not being able to live because you were not physically there to hold me up just at the right moment.

I do not remember anything about the first two days. Then they moved me to another ward, and there I looked out of the high closed windows at the sky above the Park, and I knew that I was in your hospital, and it was on that day a year ago that you had died.

I asked the young house-doctor if he had known you.

'Yes, I was taught by him last summer.'

The brash and off-hand way in which he said it. No wonder you never enjoyed lecturing to medical students. He was efficient and doing his hard job well, but how different you must have been. Where was your memorial in St Agnes's on the anniversary of your death? Why was nobody there, remembering? You, who need no memorial.

I stayed in St Agnes's for six days. Thomas came to see me. He brought me red roses. 'They are tomorrow's roses,' the flower-seller had said. Thomas was depressed. 'I am afraid you will have to live,' he said. Work, duty. I love Thomas.

How I wished that I belonged somewhere.

I would find it too difficult to write of Martin's loving concern.

I must get back to where I left off in writing to you. The hardest part is to come. I am in Zürich with Dr Frey again, who I need very much. But I must leave the Klinik soon, and continue to try. Try once more. You knew all this would happen if you died. I did not. Forgive me. I touch you with my hand tonight.

> Do not force the desert foxes from their freedom.
> Do not shoot the whining geese, whose thin lines trail the
> World. Always departing.
> Their blood will lie dark on the rose
> Of your cultivation.

*

Now, I know that those were the last days. Towards the end of July. The traffic, the dust, and the hard pavements. They were relentless, allowing no escape. Neither of us realized, then, that we had both taken on too much. There was to be no respite that year. No countryside to restore us, and to put our different problems into proportion. But had you gone away I knew I would have broken at that moment under the pressure of separation, not only for the usual reasons but because of my anxiety about your look of transparency and fragility. I would have been doubly afraid to see you go, but I knew that you ought.

'I am quite well,' you said, in answer to my repeated questions. 'You know that I always tell you when I cannot go on.'

I knew there was a great deal troubling you, and that some of it had to do with the building of your new house. I sensed that, temporarily, life was gaining over you. The size of things was becoming too great. You rarely showed it outwardly. You never showed that I had become your greatest responsibility. I believe that we had reached the point of mutual non-separation. We seemed to hold one another for different reasons. Our rules were slowly and invisibly changing, for me unconsciously, and for you? I do not know how much you knew about it.

The heat in your flat. Your window closed against the noise of the aircraft which you detested and regarded as being a hazard to people's health. The curtain drawn half-across to keep out the sun, and your electric fan turned on to keep us cool. Your piano, your books, and your plants. My chair, my footstool, and the picture of the weeds in the Cotswolds. The blue veins showing in your arms when your shirt sleeves were rolled up. The familiar smell of everything. It was the only place in the world where I wanted to be. How much I took it all for granted, while at the same time I left every evening feeling as though I might never be with those things physically again.

Thomas arranged we meet one evening. He did not come and neither did he telephone. You were so distressed for me. It was as if the disappointment had been dealt to you. I told you he was very troubled, but you said that was not a good enough reason. Once again, I saw your sense of chivalry outraged. You cared so much. I turned away and cried. You wrote a letter for me to Thomas. I would never have done that alone. I copied the words and posted them. Over how many years had he and I been painfully constant friends to one another? I forgot then. I had to wait for a reply until after the week-end. It was the time when my younger sister and her husband were having their baby christened. It was a family event which for weeks I had been dreading out of all proportion. I had been feeling increasingly ill and exhausted every day over the last month. I got through the week-end with your help. I held my third nephew and seventh god-child correctly in the church. I was glad to see my sister and her husband with a son, living in a beautiful ochre-coloured Elizabethan house surrounded by huge bushes of yew. I have no jealousy or envy of either of my sisters with their children and their husbands. Only a desperate longing, and yet – You were not sure.

I had a letter from Tom on my return, asking forgiveness, although his first words in Latin did not erase all irony. We spent an evening of happiness together in spite of his unhappiness. I think he guessed that you had written the letter. We scarcely mentioned it, but I felt that it had not displeased him. He was very aware of you, as was anyone with whom I had contact.

When I went to your flat the following evening, I felt too ill and tired to speak. It was hurting me to walk. Instead of talking, I gave you William Cowper's words from 'The Task' which I had written down especially for you that day.

> I was a stricken deer, that left the herd
> Long since; with many an arrow deep infixt
> My panting side was charg'd, when I withdrew
> To seek a tranquil death in distant shades.
> There was I found by one who had himself
> Been hurt by th' archers. In his side he bore,
> And in his hands and feet, the cruel scars.
> With gentle force soliciting the darts,
> He drew them forth, and heal'd, and bade me live.
> Since then, with few associates, in remote
> And silent woods I wander, far from those
> My former partners of the peopled scene;
> With few associates, and not wishing more.

You had never read it before, and the words seemed to move you greatly. You put the piece of paper in your desk, and closed the drawer very definitely. I felt that I had given you something at last.

I found it almost impossible to leave that evening. I knew that you had neither irritation nor anger in you. Just your wrath. Your unexploded wrath in peace; which I knew was somewhere nearer to the wrath of God than I would ever know.

When I woke the next morning, I was in such pain that I could not move. Was what I had dreaded since the previous autumn happening again? They had told me that they could never be certain it would not recur. I waited but the pain did not ease, and I telephoned you before you left for the hospital. It was the beginning of a period of nightmare, almost amounting to mental torture for both of us. And although I did not say until much later, there were not many days when I failed to remember your wife. You telephoned Mr Evans, the gynaecologist, at his home, but he was away on holiday. You arranged for an ambulance to collect me and take me to the Chelsea Hospital for Women. It came, but went away because I did not hear them ring the bell. Then you, and another ambulance and the police arrived. I managed to get to the window and throw out the key, and you sent the police away. When I saw you the pain went, and I was ashamed and embarrassed and said that the fuss was not necessary. You insisted that I go to the hospital and said you would come and see me later in the day. You took my key from me like a magpie, and put it in your pocket. It still lies in the drawer of your desk. You went to see Mrs Watson at her house in Wandsworth Bridge Road. She came at once to the hospital and I told her that I was leaving and going back to my house. I was quite all right. Then the pain returned, and once again I started to swell. The surgeon under Mr Evans came to see me. He said he would operate that morning. I telephoned you at St Agnes's, and told you that I was afraid. Once again I refused to have anything taken out which would prevent me from having a child. Once again you persuaded me to sign the piece of paper, and once again I put your name as my next of kin.

I remember you sitting beside me. I do not know whether it was that same day or the next. The surgeon said that he had removed one ovary and one fallopian tube. If he had not done so, it would have happened again in a few months. He assured me that I could still have a child. You confirmed his words over and over again until I stopped crying. Then you sat and talked about other things. I listened to your voice drifting over me and I felt your presence beside me. You talked about the woman you had been so fond of. The one who had died the previous year. You told me again how as a young man you had lodged in her house in Cresswell Place. You were so happy there, meeting many different people in an atmosphere new to you. I have already written what you told me about her. Now, you told me her name. Patricia Cousteau. Was that why you had named your daughter Patricia? You talked also of Claude, her son. You said he had once been a patient in St Agnes's; he and an Irishman had such jokes together that they had caused havoc in the hospital, paralysing the doctors and nurses with laughter. Claude Cousteau. I had met him with Martin. Antoine Cousteau, his violinist father, a friend of the Delaunay family, who Martin had known so well. Martin had had love affairs with most of the Delaunay daughters, and Gerard was so jealous that he delivered a marathon speech on Shakespeare in French, while staying at their home, L'isle Adam, in an attempt to impress and win the heart of Geneviève, the youngest.

Claude Cousteau laughing in the passages of St Agnes's. It fitted like a jig-saw puzzle. I saw a picture of your youth and an important part of your life for the first time.

Was everything breaking up?

For several days you just came and sat beside me. Whenever a nurse came into the room you told her sharply to leave. They were the only times you raised your voice. I think that they were terrified of you and did not understand who you were. Being a doctor, your position was difficult. We wished that Mr Evans was not away. We both knew him in his pin-stripe trousers, with a carnation in his buttonhole, and holding a cigarette behind his back. And after four operations he must have known my inside like his house.

Every day I waited for you to come after your work, to sit by my side and to hear your untroubled voice around me, calming, and drawing me towards you into getting well. Not until after the first days did I think of the strain upon you.

Now I know that Patricia Cousteau was a great friend of my stepmother's mother. I wish that I could talk to you about it. Another piece in the jig-saw puzzle. But it was not meant to be like that. Was it?

It had been said that life is magic. You made it so for me.

Later, Thomas came to see me every evening until he went away. We spent moments of happiness in the hospital. Sometimes he made me laugh so much that I was afraid my stitches would break, and he would leave me bathed in the perspiration of weakness.

You were happy for me about Thomas's visits. I knew that

you hoped to encounter him by mistake, but you never did. One evening, Thomas brought me an anthology. He read to me. He read me a sonnet by Mallarmé.

As I describe these last days of your life and mine together, the only thing which enables me to go on is music. In it, your thought and being come together with mine. Without it, I would not have enough meaning in my heart to continue. What will I do when it comes to an end? But there is no end to music. I have thought about that and have been discovering its truth since I was sixteen. I used to try and follow a bar of music to its end and conclusion. Once I tried to die in order to find it. I could not find its end because it lies in the Absolute. And I am not allowed. What will I do when the day comes when my writing to you ends? Perhaps it will not end in the meaning of that word. Dr Frey is going to tell me the name of a work by Mozart which comes from the same meaning as the A minor piano sonata.

Thomas was not well one evening. I took his temperature but the thermometer showed centigrade instead of fahrenheit, and neither of us knew how high it read. He telephoned me later and said that his throat was swollen and that he ached all over. He would, though, definitely come and see me or telephone the next day before he went abroad. He had decided to join his family on their holiday. He did not come, and he did not telephone. He broke off completely and went. I tried to understand. Once again you were so distressed for me. The hours we spent talking round the question. I was not strong enough to accept it then, and it put me into a deeper depression than I was already.

I do not know what I would have done without you. The interminable days. I think that I would have broken through lack of hope. That was what had happened before I met you. You were glad that you had not gone away.

'In any case I would have returned,' you said, 'and soon you will be well enough to come to my flat again.'

They always brought me my supper when you were there. I could not manage it. Hard lumps of meat lay stiff on the plate. You looked at it disapprovingly and took the tray and began to cut up the food. I see your small figure bent determinedly over the plate trying to saw the meat into appetizing pieces. A nurse came into the room, and you started, almost guiltily, and gave me back the inedible meal. When you left I wept at what seemed to me your pathos.

*

I returned to my house from the hospital with a young nurse from New Zealand. Her name was Rosita. She was making her way round the world, nursing. She was large and very healthy, and although she had the extreme friendliness of most New Zealanders, she had more the qualities of a pioneer than a nurse. She did her correct amount of hours almost too cheerfully. She talked at me about her many friends and relatives in an accent I found hard to understand. She bumped her huge frame against my bed. Each bump jarred and exhausted me, and when she moved about the whole house shook. Directly I got back I developed a fever and an infection, so painful that I could not stand up, and I was confined to bed. It went on and on, in spite of the quantities of antibiotics I took. Mrs Watson was shocked at Rosita's lack of nursing and concern, and you said without any hope in your voice: 'She is a nice enough girl, but she just has no conception of suffering in any form.'

The days grew hotter and hotter. Every afternoon Rosita went out, and you let yourself into the house with your key. The ceiling in my bedroom is low, and the white curtains against the window prevented any air from coming in. When the window was open the noise of the traffic seemed too oud for both of us, like an electric drill on our brains, so we had to close it again. You were horrified to see that I had four blankets and an eiderdown on my bed. You dragged them off one by one. You were so tired and the blankets were so heavy that you could hardly lift them.

'I will get a job as a nurse at the Chelsea Hospital for Women,' you said furiously.

The chair that you sat in was not comfortable; a fragile Sheraton gothic chair which dug into your back. Rosita broke it, bouncing up and down. I had a striped deckchair with a cushion put beside my bed. It looked strange in the room, that deckchair, but it was the only other small chair I had. My bed amused you, and that worried me out of all proportion. I detested my things to look grand or even pretty in front of you. I have written about that before. How you taught me of the total and final unimportance of material possessions in relation to other things. My bed is an exception. I made it how it is. It is a large Victorian brass bed, five feet wide. It had somehow seemed too brassy, so I painted it white. It took me three weeks. The back of the bed reaches to the ceiling and double curtains hang on either side, which increase the heat. It is a very pretty bed, nearly beautiful in its own way, but you made me feel ashamed of it.

'Where did it come from?' you asked.

'I think it came from Plymouth.'

'Yes, that post looks like an admiral's flagstaff,' you said.

You made me hate my bed, but I knew it intrigued you in a way, and that you liked to see me in it.

You would come at week-ends too, which I knew were valued times of rest for you. I was usually asleep when you came. You would wake me, and I would not greet you. I stared at you angrily which was the opposite to what I felt. I wanted to be with you so much that it had become an automatic reaction for me to create an atmosphere of resistance. I know that you understood, but it can have been no pleasure for you. You tried to persuade me to read or write, or to listen to music, but things had turned sour and stale, and I just lay in the close airless room with my pain, watching the hands of the clock move slowly round until the hour when you came. I grew to know the sound of the engine of your grey Rover car, and of your footsteps on the flights of stairs, pausing before you reached the top. You would take off your coat, and tear off your tie, and open the neck of your shirt, and quickly put them back before Rosita returned.

One Saturday morning Rosita said that there was someone to see me: 'A Mrs Wingfield.'

'I know nobody of that name,' I said.

Before I could protest a woman strode into the room. She looked overpoweringly large and business-like, and although it was not exactly a smell she exuded, it was an aroma of worldly things which one's senses only pick up in states of weakness and illness. It is a little like what animals must feel when they turn away if somebody lights a cigarette.

I put out my hand. I could not pretend to recognize her. 'I am afraid I am not sure who you are?'

'I'm Daisy. Daisy Wingfield from Dundee.'

I tried to sit up and look bright. I had met her six years before in Scotland. She was the head organizer of a Scottish charity, and I was one of the county organizers. I should have known her.

'I am so sorry to be like this when you come, but I have been in hospital. What can I offer you? A drink of some kind? You will find one in the cupboard on the landing,' I said.

She went and found some glasses and bottles. She poured two large glasses of gin, and took one to her husband who was sitting in Larissa's playroom downstairs. She settled down beside my bed. The smell of gin and of her cigarette made me pour with sweat.

'Was it a hysterectomy this time?' she asked.

I wiped my hands on the sheets. 'No, it was not.' I managed to get angry.

'Where is Larissa?'

'She is out for a walk at the moment.' I did not care what I said.

'Was the divorce difficult?'

I did not reply and she went on: 'You must come to our next annual meeting. Come to stay. You are one of our best organizers. No, not this year, but next. Royalty will be represented.'

'I am sorry to be like this but I have a fever . . . Oh, here is my doctor,' I said.

She was up and gone at the sight of you, and she went to join her husband to finish their gins. You sat with me for a long time to make sure she would not come back.

'I expect she meant well,' you said laughing. 'I think it is only people from the provinces who would call unexpectedly on someone they knew so little.'

147

We did not often laugh during those weeks. It was a bad time, wasn't it?

I had a postcard from Thomas which just showed the picture on the front and said nothing.

You were sad for me. You were wary.

You were pale and worn with work, and I knew that I was an extra strain on you. One day you were so overcome by the heat of my room that I made you drink some water, and you helped me down the stairs to the sitting-room. It was cooler there with the curtains half-drawn. There was nothing to amuse you in that room. The walls are bare, and there is only a fireplace and a table, a sofa and two armchairs. I had no need to hate it for its fantasy. I always feel as though I am in a stiff front parlour which I have deliberately refused to make into a home. It was funny how you managed to trip over things in such an empty room; the leg of a table or a chair sticking out. You would be sure to fall over something if you were not in completely familiar surroundings. You hated to lose your dignity. It was your own natural failing. I knew that it would always happen in the empty room, and I would do my best not to laugh.

That day you took off your coat and tie and shoes, and flung yourself into a comfortable chair. I had never seen you so relaxed, but it was a relaxation caused by exasperation and intense fatigue which you were unable to express. The traffic outside shook the house.

'I should think these houses are kept together by the wall-paper,' you said. 'For all they are worth.'

I had never heard that tone of mocking bitterness in your voice. I asked you about your new house.

'Oh, I am fed up with the whole thing,' you said, dismissing it.

We looked at each other across the shadowy room. We did not care at that moment whether Rosita or anyone was in the house. I could bear it no longer for myself or for you. I sat staring blankly in front of me, wondering when all this would end. You asked me if you might sit next to me on the sofa. You came, and I put my head on your chest and wept silently. I loved you then so greatly that I knew that we must surely have reached a point where our parting was near. You stroked my face and hair with a meaning in your tenderness which I had never experienced before.

'You must come to my flat tomorrow. You need to be in my room, and to get away from all this. You will come in a taxi, and I will meet you by the lift. You will manage it.'

I told you that I would come. It was the only place I wanted to be.

When the next day came I tried to stand up, but I simply could not, and I was defeated.

I seemed to get worse instead of better. I wanted to send Rosita away, but I was forced to keep her on. My fever would not go, and the doctor did nothing except to prescribe antibiotics. Being a doctor yourself, you could not interfere too much. Rosita would take no instructions from you. She only obeyed the general practitioner. My medically-minded aunt intervened, and after that the doctor came every day. I was grateful to my aunt. I could not allow my illness to go on, draining all strength from you. I asked you to send my apologies to your wife for the trouble I was causing her.

At last Mr Evans returned from his holiday. You had a discussion with him. He gave me an antibiotic which worked. My fever went. The few times you had met or talked together must have made a deep impression on him. When I was in hospital, having been moved from Zürich to London, three months after you died, he came to see me every evening for a fortnight. He just sat by my bed and chatted. At that time I needed no treatment from him. He came for a short talk. I was anxious about his fees, but he never sent me a bill. I believe that he came partly out of respect for you. Fundamentally you were both concerned, in your work, with mother and child.

You talked to me of Larissa, who was never far from our minds. You had been in regular touch with the foster-parents. You were convinced I should not let her go completely, which later I might regret so much. I should not allow my own history to repeat itself in her. 'To build happy childhood memories, that is what is so important,' you said. You told me to take everything step by step and always to keep an open mind. You would guide us. You said that you would write Larissa a letter and the reason why I had not been able to care for her myself, and how this was not through lack of loving. The letter would be for her to read when she grew up, and when she perhaps would still remember you. You never wrote it. There was no time.

One day I showed you an obituary in *The Times* of an eminent psychologist who had died in St Agnes's. You read it slowly and asked to keep it. You had known him quite well.

'I confess I did not even know that he was there,' you said, 'but what made you pay attention to this? Are you afraid that it could be mine?'

I did not answer because you had said it. I feared it so.

*

'I have decided that we must go away,' you said. 'We need it after all this. You must convalesce in the country, and I do not think that I can carry on without ten days of rest, and neither does my wife. I know of an hotel a few miles from us where you could stay. It would be quiet, and there are some lovely walks you could take, and I would come over to see you. If you agree I will arrange a room for you, and I think that you could travel by train a week from now. Rosita will have to take you there, and then she can leave.'

I was in a dubious frame of mind and I found obstacles to everything. I felt I had not the strength to move. I was grateful, but I could not understand why you should want me near to you. I put forward all kinds of difficulties.

'Of course my wife knows about it and is in agreement,' you said.

You booked a room in the hotel, and afterwards I told you that I did not think I could go. There were my sister and her husband also in the west country, and my stepmother who lived a few miles from Larissa. They had offered to have me to stay and would be hurt if I did not go. But I dreaded being thrust into the world of kind relations who did not understand you, or what your meaning was. Nor did you wish me to go to them at that moment.

The following day you came to me with another idea. You

had once taken your wife to an osteopath in the west country when she had hurt her back. A Dr Peters. He was thought to do many people good, and was also a specialist on herbs and natural foods. You were going to ask him whether he would have me to stay as a paying guest. You would come over at intervals to see me.

Again I was doubtful. What did you think of homeopaths?

You would have to drink water from the spring, and eat bread baked from stone-ground flour and all that nonsense, but it would not be for long, and they live in a nice house with a pretty garden as far as I can remember. I talked with him for some time. I thought he was a kind man although he did give me the impression that he considered we had something in common, something mutual between us, like, 'all healers we'. You laughed. You detested that sort of thing. 'You could be alone if you wanted to be, and it is only about twenty minutes' drive from where I am.'

You telephoned Dr Peters that evening. He said that he was now semi-retired, and no longer had people to stay for their health. He would try, though, to find accommodation for me near by.

'I am not going to have you staying in some bungalow in Holsbury,' you said. 'An awful little place.'

In a way I had given up. I knew that it was essential for you, and that you must go, but I would stay in the hell that my house had become, listening to the flies buzzing on the window pane, counting the days until you returned.

The next day you had a letter from Dr Peters of the Rectory, Thornworthy, in the west country. In it, he said, he had talked over the matter with Mrs Peters, and they would be very pleased to have me. You brought me, with his letter, a photograph which you had taken of the church in the village.

'Thornworthy is so small that it is really a hamlet. The church is very old and beautiful. I had to take a photograph of it. I brought it to show you because I thought that if you went you might like to go and sit there.'

I gave in, and agreed to go. We knew how tired inside the other was.

'It is a much better plan than the hotel,' you said. 'I never liked that idea. You were right. I would not have felt free to visit you there, as I will with these people. One day I will bring you over to my house so that you can see where I live. I will arrange for my wife to be out because I do not see any good coming from your meeting.'

I understood you, and understand you.

The thought of driving with you to your house, and you showing me the country; and your hill garden, and the trees and shrubs you had planted, which had dwelt for so long in my imagination, filled me with joy. To be with you in your house in the country for a brief moment had been beyond my hopes. Like a smug cat I would go alone with you.

You telephoned my sister to tell her where I was going, and explained why I was not staying with her and her husband, and you began to try bringing us together again, as we used to be. You might, you just might have achieved it, had she met you.

'What did she sound like?' I asked.

'She sounded so all right that I could not believe it was true,' you said.

I had told you before that I would like to write a letter to Karin, a Swedish girl in the Klinik, who I had met that previous Easter in Zürich. I could not do so because I had never known her other name.

'It's Malmberg,' you said. 'Write her a note. It is nice to be remembered when you are stuck in a place like that.'

'How do you know her name?' I asked.

'I had a letter from Dr Frey.' It seemed strange to me that either of you should be bothered about such details.

Your wife's brother and his wife arrived to stay with you from America. You went twice to the airport to meet them, and each time the aeroplane had been delayed. You came to see me in spite of it. I do not know how you were able to cope with their visit. I believe they were going to stay with you for a few days in the country. I think that was one of the reasons why you had so particularly wanted your garden to look in order. Was it for me too? I do not expect so.

I was fretting to know whether Thomas had returned from

his holiday. I was still unable to bear the abrupt break he had made. You were reluctant to telephone his office just to inquire if he were there, but you suggested that your brother-in-law with his American accent might do so. We both knew that it would have been a situation so absurd that we quickly abandoned the idea.

During this period that I have been writing of, our lives had been stretched to their limits. There seemed to be no more to lose. We could go on no further. The tired look of your whole being.

It was as though we were leaving for ever. The last days. I was afraid of moving; and also what the Peters would be like. You were upset and exasperated by the temporary moving of your offices while the new hospital was being built in South London. 'I made them promise from the first board meeting that they would not move me twice,' you said. When you telephoned me during the day, the noise of workmen dropping what you said were bookshelves all around you, could be heard. Disturbing your work and order, breaking the machine of your routine.

Deval and Muir (once Elkin Matthews), sellers of rare and out of print books, had sent me a postcard to say that at last they had found a copy of *The Nursing Couple*. They would forward it in due course. I had given up all hope of getting it, it appeared to be such an unobtainable book. But now I would be able to replace what I had destroyed. I gave you the postcard to show you that it was coming. You put it in your pocket.

'I will keep it as a souvenir,' you said.

You left the day before I did. You were driving to the west country. I was to go by train to Bristol with Rosita, where the Peters would meet me in their car to drive the forty miles or so to the Rectory. Rosita was to leave me at the station to make her way towards Land's End and her travels. You gave her strict instructions in front of Mrs Watson. It was true that I was still very weak.

'If the journey upsets her or makes her ill, you are to bring her straight back again on the next train,' you told her.

That was how it was. A breaking-point. If you could have,

you would have mended that breaking-point, in your room where I so long to be.

I found the country round the Rectory, Thornworthy, only rather beautiful. It was not in your territory by the sea where there must be a wildness as in Scotland. After the long drive from Bristol in Dr Peters's new car, I saw a plantation of conifers owned by the Forestry Commission. They looked unsuitable in a county of deciduous trees, and they made me suspicious of the district. Both Dr and Mrs Peters came to meet me at the station. Dr Peters was a small upright man, quick in his movements, and the look in his bright blue eyes was hard and penetrating. I felt that he was a kind man as you had said, but I had never before met anyone so opinionated. He would not have allowed anyone to question him. I wonder if he ever questioned himself? I rather doubt it. Mrs Peters was large with a loud voice and a heavily made-up face. She talked all the time, but she, too, was kind and benevolent. I soon discovered that she had once run a private nursing home. She was obedient only to Dr Peters, who called her Mrs Peters.

The Rectory did have rhododendrons somewhere. It was an old house, which they had converted and modernized. It lay in a sheltered hollow in the land surrounded by grass slopes planted with half-hardy shrubs which they tended with great care. In front of the house and the sun loggia was a circle of lawn in which grew a large clump of bamboos. The place was sunny and definitely pleasant, and the Peters did their utmost to make me welcome. Tea in the warm sun loggia. There was a home-made cake, and the stone-ground bread was good. I knew that I would never dare to smoke a cigarette. It would have been regarded as a profanity.

'If you want alcohol you have to go to the pub. The nearest one is twenty miles away!' Dr Peters joked.

I was taken round the house. They were extremely proud of what they had. Everything was in order and meticulously clean. I cannot remember what was in the pictures on the walls. There were reproductions and oils and water-colours, all of which seemed so bad that I could not look at them. Horrific would not be the right word to describe them because they were meant to please and give pleasure pleasantly. Dr Peters's study was interesting. It was the only interesting room in the house, because of his books. Apart from filing cabinets, and the couch where his patients lay to be manipulated, there was shelf upon shelf of books on medicinal herbs and plants. When I was a child, I used to brew potions out of wild plants, boiling their leaves and flowers on a fire in the birch wood in Scotland. I strained the liquid into bottles, and labelled them, and stored them secretly in neat rows. Bog myrtle, with its magical smell when the leaves are bruised, turned out to cause a festering condition when applied to a wound. I could have spent hours looking at Dr Peters's books, but it would have been out of the question. His study was closed and hallowed ground.

Dr Peters prodded me in the back, as he must have prodded his patients to feel their vertebrae. 'You are full of fear,' he said.

They had a grey clipped poodle called Barney, who they treated like their child. How I disliked that spoiled dog. I do not like poodles as a breed, even touching them, and this one had a buoyant and over-friendly nature which I was forced to pretend to admire. At supper I met the other occupants of the house. Miss Oakham, the secretary, was a silver-haired lady of a gentle sweet disposition, who had lived with the Peters for years. And then there was the beekeeper. I do not know where he fitted into the household, but he was a permanent resident, supplying them with pure honey from his hives, and working in a neighbouring town as chief apiarist for the county. He, too, was mild and shy and neutral, and I wondered how the doctor and his wife would have managed without their humble opposites. It was as though they had to have them there in order to keep at bay their own aggressive shadows. We sat at the modern refectory table in their dining-room. The water from the spring was good, as was the home-grown food. Dr Peters's conversation was sparse. It alternated between subtly-intended jokes directed at me, which made me feel uncomfortable, and not-to-be questioned reflections on the spirit and purity of all things from which the world had become so far removed. Mrs Peters kept things going with her unending and domineering chatter. She and Miss Oakham and I cleared away and washed up the supper things, before joining Dr Peters and the beekeeper in the sitting-room to watch television. A little later they had tea and biscuits. I knew that the visit was going to be a strain, but they did their best to please me. They could not have tried harder.

You telephoned me during the evening. You had to have a polite talk with Dr Peters first, and then I spoke to you in the small office which had sliding glass doors.

'Is everything all right?' you asked. 'Are you free to speak?'

'Yes, everything is all right, and thank you very much.'

You said how glad you were to be in the country, and I thought that already your voice sounded less tired. 'I will come over to see you tomorrow afternoon,' you said.

I went to bed early, before it was quite dark. A kind of homesickness was gnawing inside me amongst these kind-hearted strangers. A homesickness which perhaps I would have felt anywhere except with you. Is it not constantly with me now, in different forms? Homesickness, how well I know you, and fear you, more than physical pain.

In spite of the group of conifers amongst the deciduous greenness, I was thankful for the quietness of the country, which was only broken by the occasional clucking of a hen. I waited for sleep, and for the next day when you would come.

*

Tea was set out on the lawn by the clump of bamboos. I knew that you would not want a social occasion. You were very late. Dr and Mrs Peters and I began tea without you. I sat with my back to the front door where you would arrive. The sun shone. It was hot, but the bamboos gave a little shade. I heard your car drive up. Then you started to walk across the grass towards us. We stood up. I turned round for a moment and saw you. You were wearing grey trousers and a shirt with the sleeves rolled up. I was wearing a blue cotton shirt and a pleated skirt. Neither of us looked at one another. Mrs Peters held out a chair for you. You said that you were sorry, but the way had been longer than you had thought, and you had got lost in the lanes. 'I must have driven half way round the county,' you said. Mrs Peters cut you a piece of her fruit-cake. It lay like a brick on your plate. You broke off one small corner from it, and drank some tea. I drank milk. We did not exchange one word, and I looked in the opposite direction to you. The conversation was stilted. Even Mrs Peters seemed ill at ease and subdued in your presence and the tense atmosphere that you and I were causing. They asked you about your house. You were not really inclined to try. I knew that you were tired after your drive and losing the way, and put out by the unexpected tea-party.

You made an effort. 'The house belonged to my wife's family. It was like two huts, left over from the war, which we put together and built up. It stands on a hill overlooking the sea.'

'You must be near to Taynton Park,' Mrs Peters said.

'Yes, it is just over the river.' I saw in my mind the engraving of it hanging by your door in your flat.

'That is a lovely place,' Mrs Peters went on, 'but they say that the young Mrs Miller has spoilt it, and has taken most of the good furniture away.'

I felt you wince. You knew that Henry and Jane Miller were close friends of Maria and Richard, and that we had all been together in Italy. You made no reply. I had not contributed one word the whole time. I should have, but I could not.

Tea in a garden on a summer day with you. My dream had half come true. But it was not Dr Adler's garden, there was no interesting conversation or laughter to listen to; and there were no roses.

I turned and looked at you for the first time. You sat relaxed in your chair, toying with your piece of cake, which you then pushed aside. You were perfectly polite but you had no party manner. How I envied you and respected you for that. Between shade and sunlight, your skin looked white and transparent. You had taken off your glasses for me. Your eyes looked greener and more open than I had ever seen them. Your face, as you must have looked as a young man. Your small narrow body was thrown down, resting carelessly. We held each other's gaze, and disregarding our hosts, we were together.

Dr Peters took you for the inevitable tour of the house, and for a private talk, behaving as though you were professional colleagues. As you walked away I watched your loose graceful movements against the tight man beside you, and I knew that I had received to my full your irresistible attraction and slow charm. I saw you as a young man with whom from our very first meeting I had fallen in love. In love as much as anyone has been or can be. Did I not once hand you a sheet of paper on which I had written my dream of the night before. Something I never usually did. All that the dream had said was, 'My progress in love towards you'.

Dr Peters showed us into the sitting-room and closed the door. We sat on the brocaded sofa. Everything in the room was brocaded, and there were pots of African violets everywhere you looked.

'Can you stand it?' you asked. 'I could have done without the tea. I was not expecting all that. I came to see you.'

'I knew that you would not like it, but yes, thank you, they are very kind and do all they can to please me,' I said.

We did not feel at home in their sitting-room. Not at all.

'I quite like him, but I am not sure about her,' you said. 'It is strange, they have done so much to this house, and in many ways very well, but suddenly one comes across a picture so frightful . . . ' You half-gulped, half-laughed, and did not continue.

'It is only for ten days,' I said.

I looked at you in misery. There was no more use in hiding it from you. I could not bear for you to go away and leave me, even though you were coming back.

'I do not think that you would be happy anywhere at the moment,' you said. 'I will come again the day after tomorrow. I do not know about bringing you over to me. I know that I promised, but it is much further than I thought, and it would mean four journeys taking you there and back. A whole day's driving.'

I thought of your few days of rest and quiet. I nodded. 'Thank you for coming to see me,' I said.

'Dear Sarah, it is always nice to be thanked.'

You said that you would telephone me the following evening, and come over again the day after. Tears would not stop rolling down my face. You brushed my hand with yours, and I knew by your touch that all we had was at that moment concentrated into one whole. As you moved your arm away I heard you make an almost silent sound of pain.

'What is it?' I asked.

'Oh, nothing. I have been working hard in the garden scything bracken, and I think I have pulled a muscle,' you said.

You thought that you ought to have a few polite words with the Peters, and tell them your plans before you left. You looked at my face.

'I do not want to see them,' I said.

'No, don't.'

'Shall I go up to my room?' I asked you.

'Yes, I would go to your room.'

I hit my head hard against your chest. It was my way of parting. How often have I reproached myself that it was not entirely without anger? I did not look at you again. I walked up the stairs holding tightly on to the banister, leaving you behind me.

I spent the next day taking a short walk up the lane towards the church of which you had taken a photograph. Although it was so near to the Rectory, I was too tired to reach it. I sat in the sun spinning out the beautiful day, smelling the purple flowers of the buddleia in the garden, and laying the table for supper in the dining-room. I could not read. I waited for the evening when you would telephone me.

After washing up the supper things we watched television again. I did not concentrate on the programme. The telephone rang. I wondered if it were you. Dr Peters had many calls. He answered it, and returned beckoning me with his finger saying there was a message for me. He showed me to the office and pulled out a chair. I did not like the way in which he did it. His exaggerated abruptness made me uneasy. I picked up the receiver of the telephone and said: 'Hello' expecting to hear your voice. Instead I heard a woman say my name. I did not know her voice. It was very clear and sweet, speaking slowly as with great difficulty. I felt fear surge, and immediately I knew. Your wife could have been spared her task by just saying my

name. What I had dreaded most in my world, my life, my soul
and existence on earth, had now happened.

'My husband died this afternoon. He had a heart attack. He
was working in the garden and collapsed. He died within a few
minutes. Today he had said that he had decided to bring you
over here and that we should meet. I am with him now, beside
him. I wanted to tell you myself.'

She tried to control her voice and say words of help and
understanding but I did not hear them. I said over and over
again, 'I am so sorry for you.' It was all I could say for her who
I had never met. I did not exist. Only she. The telephone was
replaced. Everything was dark, and there was no light inside
me.

I found my way back to the Peters to tell them I was going
upstairs to my room. They held me back saying that I was to
stay with them. In the shadowy gloom of the television. They
would not allow me to go. An hysterical sobbing came over me
and Mrs Peters tried to clasp me to her. Her body was large and
soft and warm, but I struggled to free myself. They held me
down like an animal, pushing minute pills down my throat. I
saw the little beekeeper leave the room. He could not bear it.
Between moments of harsh reality and nightmarish unreality,
between consciousness and unconsciousness I felt compassion
for him, and the sadness I sensed in his life. I felt compassion
for every living thing, and most of all for your wife. I think
Mrs Peters put me to bed. She would not allow me to take a
sleeping pill. She put a glass tube of the round white pills beside
me and told me to take those. They were made from the roots
of a South American plant and would act as a sedative. I cried
no longer, but I had no control over my body. I was freezing
cold and I shook all over. A silence had come over everything
and a terror. Mrs Peters sat with me for a while and then left.
I begged her not to turn out the light in the passage. I lay awake
all night trembling with fear because I knew and at the same
time did not know what had happened. I believed it and did not
believe it. At times when the trembling stopped, I found that I
could not breathe. I gasped and fought for my breath like an
asthmatic. It went on and on, and I staggered round the room

trying to get air into my lungs, and then fell again on to the bed. How I wish my heart had stopped then as it was trying to do. I must have slept towards dawn because I remember waking and experiencing the feeling common to most bereaved people, and one which was to come every morning. It is the knowledge that some overwhelming disaster has taken place, and you are not aware what it is. Then consciousness comes and the great heaviness which has been weighing upon you draws aside, and reality takes its place to stand before you. If you cannot feel God within you, the sun does not rise any more.

The day after you died was another late summer day. The blue sky, and the green fields, and the trees with their lengthening shadows. How were they able to remain unchanged without you? I saw the sun turn black. I wept, and nothing happened, and you did not come.

*

In the darkness, knowing but not knowing, I continued to function. I wrote to your wife and said all that I could for her. I grieved for her more than myself.

I told the Peters that must return to London. I had no idea where I was going but I think it was to your room. The Peters told me that I had to remain with them.

'It was his wish that you should stay with us until you were well,' they said.

At first I felt sorry for them, that they should have been put in such a situation. They too, were shocked and they spoke in low-pitched voices together, talking of things I guessed, but could not hear. There was nothing I could do, and no source of comfort to turn to, except to hold my small wooden image of Christ with its aromatic scent. You used to admire it, and I would make you smell it, and we wondered why a carving from ordinary olive wood should so persistently, perhaps for over two hundred years, give out this powerful sweet bitterness which increases in the warmth of your hand.

It was August bank holiday, and your funeral was delayed.

You wife telephoned me again and thanked me for my letter, and said would I still like to come to the house as you had intended. I wanted to so much, just for one brief moment to see your garden, the place where you had died, and where your body had lain. To make it real for myself. I never went. Your wife did not mention it again. I think it would have been too much for her to bear. She said that she wished to meet me. Neighbours were taking care of her, and they drove her one morning over to the Rectory. I saw her alone in my room. We confronted each other tentatively. We wanted to meet but at the same time feared it. Our meeting was close but also far apart. She looked and behaved as I had always imagined her; like a good mother instead of the suffering grieving woman she was. She sat on the chair and I sat on the floor. She explained to me exactly what had happened which I have written at the beginning of my writing to you. How during the last day you had been talking and wondering about life after death, something you rarely spoke of. That you did not know how you were going to be able to return to the noise and turmoil of London. How you called to her as you fell, and that she had tried to revive you by giving you the kiss of life. But it was in vain. Your heart had stopped. They said that the look in your eyes then had been of joy and discovery. Who in the world can discount it? Only you.

Your wife went on to say that you had never been able to help your own daughter, but you knew that you could help me, and your greatest wish was that I should get well. She said that she would keep in touch with me, and watch over Larissa's progress as her husband would have wished.

'He would be so angry with himself for dying,' she said. She had had the thoughtfulness and presence of mind to bring me some sleeping pills. I cannot forget the control she had over herself during our meeting. She was in a state of shock, and I knew at breaking-point, but stayed calm and brave the whole time. Her world had vanished within a few short seconds; to the outside, far more than mine. There was nothing that I could do for her except to be well and strong, thereby lifting one burden off her mind. Instead I sat listening to her with tears streaming down my face. They were for her. She had her own great sorrow and tragedy which would never leave her, but she had lived through your dying. She had felt, seen, and touched it. She was surrounded by the things you saw, and felt, and touched. She had the necessary work and action connected with you to keep her going, and your daughter and your brother were arriving to be with her. She could mourn with a family who loved you, and she had your body to cherish and to bury. Was that where her strength lay?

After the visit of your wife, the Peters decided that the time for mourning was over. Things in their household and for me should be restored as near as possible to normal. I tried my hardest to help them, and to behave as they expected me to. I laid the table, and sat at meals, washed up, and walked up and down the stairs, but my tears would not cease streaming and streaming. I tried to smile and to make conversation, but my tears went on and on. I was isolated. I could not talk to the Peters.

'No person should depend on another,' said Dr Peters. 'It is against the law of God and nature.'

'His wife is a wonderful example,' said Mrs Peters. 'She has taken it so much in her stride.'

How could I tolerate their words, and their talk about the spirit, mixed with innocuous tales of fun? I could no longer stand the Peters, their house, their dog — their whole environment. I moved automatically, weeping silently day and night. I knew that I must get away, but I was waiting for your funeral to which I was not to go. I longed so much to be there, to live through it, to complete a circle which would then have no end. But I had no place. It was to be for the family. I had no way to express my mourning for you. I was locked up and imprisoned — stunned in my lonely grief, and unable even to give you flowers.

I began a period of action to break the tension and unreality. I telephoned Thomas at his office. He told me to get in touch with him as soon as I got back to London. I telephoned Dr Frey in Zürich. It was not really for me to tell him of your death. Was it? What would you say? I knew that he would wish to be told, and also I knew that I would have to reach him in Züurich as quickly as possible before the crash came which I was trying my hardest to prevent. I fought against it. I did not think about it but I must have felt it advancing nearer and nearer.

'I have got bad news for you,' I said to Dr Frey. I told him what had happened.

'When?'

Again I told him.

'It was the heart?'

'Yes,' I said.

He asked me where he could write to your wife. I said that she was going to stay with friends before she returned to the flat, but the letter would reach her if he wrote to the London address. I asked him if I could come and see him within a few days.

I told the Peters that I would shortly be leaving them for Zürich, to see a friend of yours who owned a clinic. I think that they secretly distrusted psycho-analysis. They did not say so, but they definitely regarded our relationship as an unnatural phenomenon. They were treating me with their homeopathic pills. They refused to let me go until the originally agreed time with them was up. Did they know the torture that they were inflicting on me? I do not think so. They had such implicit faith in themselves.

As I sat on the circle of lawn in the afternoon, I saw a woman coming quickly towards me, and as though she were not sure of her surroundings. Her outline looked familiar, and suddenly I realized that it was my stepmother. I threw myself into her arms, as I just might have done when my father had been alive. At last to see a face I knew. She had not liked to come, thinking that I would not wish to see her, but my aunt had ordered her to go. The next day she drove the long distance again from where she lives, and took me for a picnic in a lane. I remember talking wildly to her, just talking and talking of death. We discussed for the first time the hostility which had existed between us since my father's death. It could be said that I had tried to comfort her then, she did the same for me now. As far as our different personalities would allow, we were reconciled. It has lasted. I wonder what you would say? As for me and my family: I love them warily. Far apart, and near if they were to need me.

My stepmother talked with the Peters and told them politely but firmly that she would be taking me away the next day.

'She will be going straight to Zürich,' she said.

They agreed reluctantly. Did they imagine they were failing to do their duty? 'It was not the plan,' they said.

Miss Oakham, the secretary, was growing excited. She was leaving for her holiday in a few days' time. She was going on a tour of Switzerland.

'Just think, we will be there at the same time,' she said.

Gentle, sympathetic Miss Oakham. I shall not forget her. I smiled at her and said: 'So we will,' and the tears went on pouring down my face.

*

Writing to you has become so hard and painful that for the last two days I have felt a deep depression. I must finish my writing, this particular writing to you – I must pause, though, before I can go on to describe what lately has had so much, and yet so little to do with you. I feel as though I am living again those first days without you. The days which had, but had not, to do with you.

The other day I placed a razor blade on the sofa in what they call here the therapy room. It lay between Dr Frey and myself. I put it there to show him what I felt.

'That is the river between us,' I said, pointing to it. 'You are the enemy on the one side, and I am the enemy on the other. I am also the enemy on both sides.'

When we had finished talking about other things, he put the sharp blade in his pocket with a movement as though he were doing something else. They searched my belongings without my knowing it and took away everything dangerous. Dr Frey was in the Klinik during that afternoon. I was writing to you. I did not know that he was there, but he came up behind me, and I felt his hands on my shoulders. I did not look at him.

'Are you managing?' he asked.

'No.'

'Try again,' he said. Then he walked away.

I wish that I had looked at him.

Late at night I went into the bathroom and took the broken pieces of a razor blade which I had kept. I slashed my wrist again and again, as deeply as I could. I knew perfectly well that it would not kill me, not like the times before. They have been something quite different. As my writing to you comes to a close, the pain is so unbearable inside me that a force of such strength has driven me to inflict a physical pain on myself in the hope of appeasing the other. Herr Stieler, who was on night-duty, found me with the blood dripping into the bath. I felt sorrow towards him. But to feel sorry is not enough for violence, in any form. And yet, again and again.

I now continue to write to you, strapped in bed, and with my wrist bound in bandages. What low endurance – do not despise me.

*

On the day of your funeral I received the obituary of you from *The Times*. I say to you, how bald and sparing of epithets it is. No reader, who did not know you, could guess what lay behind the cold inhuman words – like those on a railway ticket – 'Not transferable'. But yes, is it not right and suitable for you, who would have shied from a public eulogy? What do such things mean anyway? And yet – yes, how thankless.

Your cremation was held in the nearest town. Do you have no grave? You would not have cared at all, perhaps you would not have wished for one; it is only I, in my chained and restricted body, who long for a memorial to see and to touch.

I went to evensong in the small church at Thornworthy. I was going to your funeral. The same day and the same time. The five-minute bell was ringing too quickly and too impatiently for tolling. The church looked just the same as in the photograph you had taken. I walked up the path, through the cemetery which was filled with ancient graves. The church door creaked when I opened it. Inside, the smell was of antiquity. The church pews creaked when you moved.

You had said that you thought that the church was a place I might like to go and sit alone.

How many times had Mrs Watson said to me over the years: 'In the midst of life we are in death.' I had always known it perfectly well.

As I sat in the empty church I knew that you had been there, and that it had remained vividly in your memory. For the first time I felt your presence faintly. The sun penetrated the closed cool church, and one shaft lay across the flagstone floor. The organist came in and took his place, turning over the pages of music as though he could not decide what to play. Perhaps he did not know many pieces. There were two other members of the congregation. An old man with a young boy beside him. We made three in all. The organist began to play. The music was nearly drowned by the sound of the pumping of the bellows. On the altar the candles were lit, and there were two small vases of flowers on either side of the cross in the middle. I did not take my eyes from the altar covered in its embroidered cloth. I imagined your coffin lying before it, and your body which I so much loved. I did not say the prayers, or sing the hymns and psalm, and neither did I listen to the short sermon. I watched with my face drenched in tears. For the first time they were not coming from the heat of the salt desert inside me.

The old man, and the boy, and the clergyman all glanced at me. Who was this stray holiday-maker? But they turned their eyes away. I did not wish to embarrass them. They did not know that I was attending the burial of the dead. Afterwards, the clergyman standing by the door shook my hand, and was about to speak, but not knowing what to say, he turned as if to greet his imaginary parishioners following behind me.

I had heard some of the evensong. I listened to what I had been waiting for. I waited for the Nunc Dimittis to be sung for you. Would you find that it said too much? Like music without any silence or rests. I do not believe so. 'Lord, now lettest thou thy servant depart in peace: according to thy word. For mine eyes have seen: thy salvation; Which thou hast prepared: before the face of all people; . . . As it was in the beginning, is now, and ever shall be: . . . without end.'

*

In my writing I am always afraid of saying too much. I know how you would dislike it. I have not written of things which cannot be written, but what I have written is the truth. What I write to you will never be complete, but before I reach the present time I must tell you fragments of what has happened.

My stepmother took me the evening of your funeral to spend one night in her house. The next morning, on our way to catch the train to London, we drove through the town where Larissa goes to school. I was afraid that I would see her.

I went to my house for one hour. Thomas came to see me. He was at a loss what to say. 'I am afraid I was not very much help to you,' he wrote me afterwards. I think it was beyond his understanding. Most of the people I know think it was just a broken transference in the realm of psycho-analysis. A big loss and shock, but nothing real. They do not know that the greatest human love that I shall ever give or receive has gone from me. I cannot speak of it. It is not allowed. It increases the loneliness.

Mrs. Watson wept. She never looks at the list of deaths in the newspaper, but had happened to do so that day.

Martin read it in Baden-Baden. He said that he had immediately returned to London, but thought that I would not wish to see him. At that moment he thought correctly. It would have been a betrayal to you. Things are different with him now, but I am always wary of a certain element, stealthily coming.

I could not stop weeping in the streets of London. I tried harder and harder to exercise self-control, but it had abandoned me. I scarcely knew what I was doing amongst the people and the traffic. The city fell all around me. The crash I feared was coming.

I read over and over again, in search of some sort of comfort, an Egyptian poem. It reminded me of you.

> Death is before me today,
> Like the recovery of a sick man,
> Like going forth into a garden after sickness;
> Death is before me today,
> Like the odour of myrrh,
> Like sitting under the sail on a windy day;

Death is before me today,
Like the odour of lotus flowers,
Like sitting on the shore of drunkenness;
Death is before me today,
Like the course of the freshet,
Like the return of a man from the war-galley to his house,
When he has spent years in captivity.

When I arrived at the Klinik in Zürich, I was put to bed in the therapy room. I do not remember correctly about that period of time. Images come and go, in sections of memory.

I remember looking out of the window of the therapy room towards the garden. Dr Frey was behind me. Suddenly the trees and the grass and the flowers started to tremble. I could see the outline and vein in every leaf and petal as though under a magnifying-glass. Their trembling stopped as suddenly as it had begun, and a petrified silence descended upon them. Their minute detail grew and grew as though they were going to engulf me, and their colours shone and blazed before my eyes. Perhaps that is how the world would look if our eyes were opened? The trees and flowers in the suburban garden appeared in such threatening beauty that no ordinary nature as mine could have stood it.

If only I could hold and touch your body and to bury it.

I could not stop the breaking-down – like someone mad whose mind is smashed. Dr Frey was waiting behind me. He took me upstairs and I was put to bed and given an injection.

I took medicine every day – more and more. I could not stop the weeping, neither could I stand the world without you. The medicine made me so tired that I just lay all the days in the garden by the clump of bamboos, or on the balcony in the September sun, putting a blanket and a pillow on the tiled floor to lie on, making a place for myself. I read but I could not remember what I had read. I wrote letters and received many too. People were very kind. Your wife sent me several letters which I have kept for their remarkable and unselfish words. She sent me the photograph of you which I look at so many times a day, and take with me wherever I go.

I had meals downstairs in the dining-room. Zack, Karin,

Jeremy Rowell, Lechleitner, Erik, Judy, Verena – all of them were still there. I had not thought I would come back. I had sworn that I never would. To my shame I cried at meals. 'You are taking too much medication,' Lechleitner said. When I stopped crying I began to break things. I smashed a window with a bottle and was moved to the first floor in the room with Frau Prawitt, and Solange, and the red-haired Margareta.

I do not remember very much more. Just some pictures, snatches of the days. I developed a high fever. I wanted to die and not to go on living without you. My body wanted to die. My blood cells went wrong. I became swollen all over. My eyes and ears were closed. My hair was matted and tied in plaits because the sisters could not comb or wash it. I was covered in disease. I became delirious. They were all very kind. I remember Schwester Elise trying to feed me soup, spoon after spoon. Voices singing 'Happy Birthday'. I did not know that it was mine. A bunch of flowers and ivy, which they told me was from Martin. A goldsmith cutting off my wedding-ring which is engraved with ferns and ivy; my hands were so swollen that they could not pull it off. I did not want them to cut my wedding ring. There was a moment . . .

> Was it a dream? We sailed, I thought we sailed,
> Martin and I, down a green Alpine stream,
> Bordered each, bank, with pines; the morning sun,
> On the wet umbrage of their glossy tops,
> On the red pinings of their forest – floor,
> Drew a warm scent abroad; behind the pines
> The mountain – skirts, with all their sylvan change
> Of bright-leafed chestnuts and mossed walnut – trees
> And the frail scarlet-berried ash, began.
> Swiss chalets glittered on the dewy slopes,
> And from some swarded shelf, high up, there came
> Notes of wild pastoral music – over all
> Ranged, diamond-bright, the eternal wall of snow.*

Why cannot I describe my illness? Because it is so uninteresting. Because it was another time of hell. I have to write of it

---

*Matthew Arnold, *Early Poems*. A Dream.

though because it happened. I thought that Schwester Adolphine was a member of the Gestapo, and I cried when she entered the room. 'It is a day of penitence,' she said. I was afraid that they would put me in a cell. But Dr Frey said that they had no cells. Dr Frey went away on holiday. Solange nearly set her bed on fire, and they took away her cigarettes and matches. Frau Prawitt, the old, old lady, did crayon drawings in beautiful clear colours, and walked around the room at night whispering to herself in the dark. Lechleitner read a psalm over me. He thought that I was going to die. Shall we laugh? It was in Latin. Then there was a blankness, except for the vague knowledge of Dr Pestalozzi looking at me through his quizzing-glass, and someone dropping me into the back of an ambulance.

I do not remember the Kantonsspital until some days after my arrival. They thought I would die, but they stopped me. They injected me with cortisone and painted me all over with a purple dye, and bound my whole body in linen bandages. They would not allow me to sit up in case I saw my disfigured face in the looking-glass. The disease went inside me, and I could not swallow, so they attached my arm to a glucose and water drip. I did not weep any more. My mind had become anaesthetized. I had no tears or feeling left. All I sensed was the pain and stench of my body with its weeping skin. It was when I knew that they were not going to let me die that the fear came. Cortisone makes one alert and nervous. I lay awake throughout the nights listening for the trams to start at half-past five. Sips of valerian in the dark was all I was allowed. Schwester Elise came to see me. She lent me her watch because I had destroyed my clock. My stepmother came to be with me. I shall always be grateful to her. Dr Frey returned from his holiday. He had thought that I was still in the Klinik. He sat by my bed in the Kantonsspital. He wore his bright blue jersey. I was glad to see him, but I felt as though I had done something wrong. I do not know why. I would not return to the horrors of the Klinik. I wanted to go home, but I did not know where that was. The draw-strings of Dr Frey pulled me to and fro. I knew that he knew about some of your secrets. What would I have done if you had not sent me to Dr Frey?

I did after all return to London; in a wheel chair because I could hardly walk. Two weeks in hospital. Your wife came to see me as soon as I arrived, and several times after. She did it for you. 'It's all part of it,' she said. At that time I almost clung to her in my weakness. But our meetings were never easy. The bond which we tried to make has been broken gently, and I believe thankfully. The only help I can give her is to remain away from her, and stay well, giving meaning to your work.

The only means I have of thanking Dr Frey is by giving him my trust, as I have done in this writing to you; and also to go on.

After two weeks in the hospital I went to be with my step-mother in the country. I tried very hard not to return to Zürich, but then the pain inside me started again, and I had to go back to Dr Frey. I have told you all the rest. I am leaving the Klinik again this week. I have been here this time for a month. I have been in the room with the balcony, sharing with Judy, and Frieda, and Fräulein Keller. I have not been outside at all. I have stayed to finish this incomplete and inadequate writing to you. I do not feel the ground sure beneath my feet. I hope that Dr Frey will not leave me as in a broken friendship. He is one of my closest friends now – really – even more than the few good friends I have. He is a stern Swiss Herr Doktor.

Since you died, I have tried myself to die three times. Once naturally, and twice by my own hand. Each time I have so nearly succeeded. I know that I must live. I would like to visit Larissa soon. I repeat that I must live. I do not disregard duty. I must work in whatever my capacity. What is my capacity? Where does it lie? To work, to do? My strength?

I see you walk up the steps of the Klinik, taking your hat off as you approach the front door. They are going to pull down the Hotel Waldhaus Dolder. You are part of this place. I cry and weep inside me. I can give you no promise that I will make it without you, as you would so wish me to. I will gather my will-power and training, and remember all you taught me, but I am forced to admit that it is not entirely in my own hands. I will try once more. I speak like one who asks forgiveness again and again. In my weakness I am not thankless. Please believe me.

It is my greatest fear that I will fail, in order to try to be with you. I must wait until I am allowed.

You who gave the world all you had, not merely to justify your existence, but because you cared for it more than your own life.

They who knew you thought, if they thought at all, that without you cities would not fall.

Those close to you knew that their lives would never be the same again.

And sometimes I forget that you gave to me your heart. For ever. You said.

> Once, when young,
> I found a shrine in the hill
> Built by no one.
> The altar which received me
> There, remains. Still
> One hand high.